1965

THE NEWS
THE EVENTS
AND
THE LIVES
OF 1965

WILLIAM DEAN & ELIZABETH ABSALOM

Published by D'Azur Publishing 2024
D'Azur Publishing is a Division of D'Azur Limited

Copyright © D'Azur Publishing 2024
William Dean and Elizabeth Absalom have asserted his rights under the Copyright, Design and Patents Act 1988 to be identified as the author of this work.

The language, phrases and terminology within this book are as written at the time of the news reports during the year covered and convey and illustrate the sentiments at that time, even though modern society may find some words inappropriate. The news reports are taken from internationally recognised major newspapers and other sources of the year in question. The language does not represent any personal view of the author or publisher.

All Rights Reserved. No part of this publication may be reproduced, stored or transmitted in any form or by any means, electronic, mechanical, digital or otherwise, except under the terms of the Copyright, Designs and Patents Act 1988 or under terms of a licence issued by the publisher. This book is sold subject to the condition that it shall not, by way of trade or otherwise, be lent, resold or hired out, or otherwise circulated without the publishers prior consent in any form or binding or cover other than that in which it is published and without a similar condition, including this condition, being imposed on the subsequent purchaser.
All requests to the Publisher for permission should be addressed to info@d-azur.com.

First published in Great Britain in 2024 by D'Azur Publishing
Contact: info@d-azur.com Visit www.d-azur.com
ISBN 9798301827983

ACKNOWLEDGEMENTS
The publisher wishes to acknowledge the following people and sources:

Series Editor Elizabeth Absalom. Additional Research by Amanda Dean; British Newspaper Archive; The Times Archive; Cover Malcolm Watson; p8 (crowd) Tim Toomey on Unsplash; p10 (Big Ben) Squirrel_photos from Pixabay; p10 (Concorde) By Eduard Marmet; p10 (Carnival) Marie0771; p14 (Chernobyl) IAEA Imagebank - p15 (Catchphrase) By ITV - itv.com; p20 (Earthquake) courtesy of NOAA; p27 By Traced from a brochure. Colours modified to reflect logo version from 2009., p27 (waves) Image by Didier from Pixabay; p29 mini; p47 Jurassica02; p53 (toothbrush) Napoleon Bonaparte's Toothbrush. Wellcome Collection. Source: Wellcome Collection; p53 Nelson's spy-glass and tourniquet used in the amputation of his arm at Tenerife, 1797. Wellcome Collection. Source: Wellcome Collection;p53 A certain cure for the bite of a mad dog / R. M. Source: Wellcome Collection; p57 Philip Allfrey; Sodacan - Own work; p63 (Runnymede View) By WyrdLight.com; p69 Malcolm Watson; p77 (Smith) Koch, Eric for Anefo neg. stroken; p81 (mountain) Malcolm Watson; p95 (Schweitzer) By Bundesarchiv, Bild p109 (Plaque) Nick Harrison; p121 (street lights) Jeffrey Zhang on Unsplash;

Whilst we have made every effort to contact copyright holders, should we have made any omission, please contact us so that we can make the appropriate acknowledgement.

CONTENTS

1965 Highlights Of The Year					4-5

1965 The Year You Were Born					6-7

1970 The Year You Were Five					8-9

1976 The Year You Were Eleven					10-11

1981 The Year You Were Sixteen					12-13

1986 The Year You Were Twenty One				14-15

1965 The Major Sporting Events					16-17

1965 The Major Cultural Events					18-19

1965 Science and Nature						20-21

1965 The Lifestyles of Everyday People				22-23

THE YEAR DAY-BY-DAY						**24-127**

The 1965 calendar						128

Life In 1965

Monarch: Queen Elizabeth II

Prime Minister: Harold Wilson (Labour)

In 1965 Britain, Harold Wilson was presiding over a country where the first 'baby boomers' were due to come of age and were intent on personal freedom and permissiveness. It was the year Sir Winston Churchill dies; Sir Stanley Matthews plays his last first division game; cigarette adverts are banned from British television; Goldie the golden eagle has 13 days of freedom from London Zoo; Ian Smith declares UDI in Rhodesia and Pizza Express and Kentucky Fried Chicken open in Britain.

The first English National Trail, the Pennine Way, gave walkers access to some of the country's wildest landscapes from the Peak District hills in Derbyshire to the Scottish Borders with a *combined* ascent that exceeds the height of Mount Everest. Brothers Ronnie and Reggie Kray are arrested on suspicion of running a protection racket in London; for the first time in their history Liverpool win the FA Cup and (CSE) Certificate of Secondary Education is introduced in schools.

The Pennine Way

FAMOUS PEOPLE WHO WERE BORN IN 1965

5th Jan: Vinnie Jones, footballer and actor
14th Jan: Hugh Fearnley-Whittingstall, chef
15th Jan: James Nesbitt, Northern Irish actor
30th Mar: Piers Morgan, tabloid journalist
3rd May: Rob Brydon, comedian and actor
10th Jun: Elizabeth Hurley, model and actress
31st Jul: J. K. Rowling, English author
2nd Sep: Lennox Lewis, boxer
12th Dec: Will Carling, English rugby player

FAMOUS PEOPLE WHO DIED IN 1965

4th Jan: T. S. Eliot, poet, Nobel Prize laureate
24th Jan: Winston Churchill, Statesman
23rd Feb: Stan Laurel, English comic film actor
28th Mar: Richard Beesly, British Olympic gold medal rower
11th Nov: James Chuter Ede, Labour politician,
25th Nov: Dame Myra Hess, English pianist
22nd Dec: Richard Dimbleby, journalist and broadcaster

News Of The Year

JANUARY — Ronnie and Reggie Kray, identical twins, are arrested on suspicion of running a London protection racket but are acquitted In April.

FEBRUARY — National Health Service prescription charges are abolished by the Wilson Government.

MARCH — 'Goldie', a golden eagle flew away from his keepers while his cage was being cleaned and escaped from London Zoo. He was finally captured after thirteen days of freedom.
The first Pizza Express restaurant opens in London.

APRIL — The Finance Act comes into force, introducing corporation tax for businesses.

MAY — KFC the fast-food restaurant chain opens its first branch in Preston, Lancashire.

JUNE — In a clampdown on drink driving, the government announces plans to introduce a blood alcohol limit for drivers. Exceeding these limits can result in fines and bans.
The school-leaving qualification Certificate of Secondary Education (CSE) is first examined.

JULY — The Secretary of State for Education and Science, requests local authorities to convert their secondary schools to the Comprehensive system.

AUGUST — Cigarette advertising is banned from British television.

SEPTEMBER — With security in the British Protectorate of Aden worsening, the Governor cancels the Aden constitution and takes direct control.

OCTOBER — Ian Brady and Myra Hindley are charged with three murders. 150 police officers search Saddleworth Moor for the bodies of up to 11 missing children.

NOVEMBER — The Abolition of Death Penalty Act suspends capital punishment for murder.

DECEMBER — The Race Relations Act makes it a civil offence to discriminate on the grounds of colour, race, ethnicity or nationality and creates the offence of "incitement to racial hatred".
A 70-mph speed limit is imposed on UK roads.

Films and Arts

At the height of Beatlemania, the 'fab four' release and star in their film, **Help!** Julie Christie stars in the romantic drama, **Darling,** with Dirk Bogarde and Laurence Harvey. **The Sound of Music**, starring Julie Andrews becomes an enormous box office hit. It is based on the stage musical composed by Richard Rodgers with lyrics by Oscar Hammerstein.

The unknown Tom Jones took **It's Not Unusual** to the No1 slot after singer Sandie Shaw heard it as a demo and thought he was too good to give it up! **Round the Horne** made its debut on BBC Radio staring Kenneth Horne, Kenneth Williams, Hugh Paddick, Betty Marsden and Bill Pertwee.

The children's television series **Jackanory** airs on the BBC. It was designed to stimulate an interest in reading. The first story was the fairy-tale "Cap-o'-Rushes" read by Lee Montague. **Jackanory** broadcast around 3,500 episodes over 30 years. **The Magic Roundabout** makes its debut.
New books this year included Ian Fleming's James Bond novel **The Man with the Golden Gun** and John Fowles's novel **The Magus.**

1965 THE YEAR

Born in 1965, you were one of 54.2 million people living in Britain and your life expectancy *then* was 71.3 years. You were one of the 17.7 births per 1,000 population and you had a 2% chance of dying as an infant, a rapidly declining chance as this figure in 1950 was almost 3.1%. People had become used to post-war affluence, but the economy was not without its crises. Whilst many enjoyed the 'swinging sixties' there was still real poverty in many city centres and tower block, 'streets in the sky', living was becoming less and less popular, many areas deteriorating and experiencing rising crime.

The first female High Court judge was appointed. The Race Relations Act is passed; the National Viewers' and Listeners' Association is founded by Mary Whitehouse; Sir Winston Churchill dies; Corgi Toys introduce the all-time best-selling model car, James Bond's Aston Martin DB5 from the film Goldfinger.

How Much Did It Cost?

The Average Pay:	£932 (£18 p.w.)
The Average House:	£3,092
Loaf of White Bread:	1s 2½d (6p)
Pint of Milk:	9d (4p)
Pint of Beer:	2s 3d (11p)
12mnths Road Tax	£15
Gallon of Petrol:	5s 1d (6p/litre)
Newspapers:	5d - 1s (2-5p)
To post a letter in UK:	3d (1p)
TV Licence	£5 Black & White

The Magic Roundabout made its debut on BBC television using footage of an original French animation show, but with completely different scripts, written in English for the British audience, and told by Eric Thompson. Although the characters are common to both versions, they were given different names and personalities depending on the language. The show goes on to attain 'cult status'.

YOU WERE BORN

POPULAR CULTURE

Round the Horne made its debut on BBC Radio. Kenneth Horne, Kenneth Williams, Hugh Paddick, Betty Marsden and Bill Pertwee introduced the nation to the larger than life, 'Julian and Sandy', 'J. Peasmold Gruntfuttock' and 'Rambling Syd Rumpo', all with abounding 'double entendres'.

Paul McCartney of The Beatles records the song Yesterday at Abbey Road Studios in London and husband and wife duo, Sonny (Bono) and Cher made their debut with a No 1 hit, I Got You Babe.

Both Cilla Black and the Righteous Brothers had a hit with You've Lost That Lovin' Feelin' but only the Americans took it to No1 whilst Ken Dodd's Tears is officially recorded as the biggest selling single of the year, staying at the top of the hit parade for five weeks.

Where Are You Now (My Love) was written by Tony Hatch and Jackie Trent and gave Trent her only No1 hit. It was featured in the TV series It's Dark Outside.

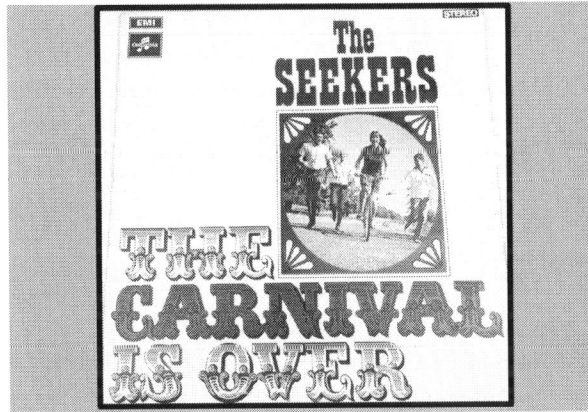

Australian group The Seekers had three top 10 entries in their breakthrough year, including the number-one singles I'll Never Find Another You and in December, The Carnival is Over one of the biggest-selling singles of all time.

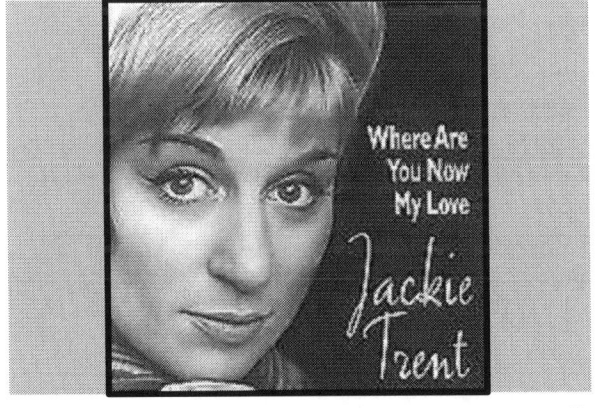

7

1970 The Year

In 1970, Edward Heath, Conservative, took over from Harold Wilson, Labour, and continued to preside over a period of huge social, cultural and political changes. This year the age of majority is reduced to 18; the half-crown coin and ten-shilling note cease to be legal tender; the first jumbo jet to land in England, a Boeing 747, lands at Heathrow Airport; The Sun newspaper has its first appearance of a Page Three girl.
Also, the Apollo 13 mission failed, but miraculously the spacecraft returned to earth, and all the crew survived. The US invaded Cambodia, and thousands of Americans protested in Washington. The Beatles shocked the music world by announcing they were disbanding, and the music festival on the Isle of Wight drew a record 600,000 crowd.

Five In 1970

School started for children at 5 years old and the day was filled with basic education – reading, writing, numeracy, nature study, music and art. Many junior schools now insisted on a school uniform like their senior counterparts.

Children were free to play outside without supervision when not at school, coming in for meals or bedtime and the NERF ball, marketed as the 'the first indoor ball' was the toy every child wanted this year.

How Much Did It Cost?

The Average Pay:	£1,600 (£32 p.w)
The Average House:	£4067
Loaf of White Bread:	1s 6d (7p)
Pint of Milk:	1s (5p)
Pint of Beer:	2s 11d (15p)
12mnths Road Tax	£25
Gallon of Petrol:	6s (30p)
Newspapers:	5d - 1s (2-5p)
To post a letter in UK:	5d (2p)
TV Licence	£6 Black & White £12 Colour

You Were Five

Popular Culture

The Six Wives of Henry VIII is first broadcast, on BBC2, whilst Jon Pertwee makes his first appearance as the Third Doctor in Doctor Who, and A Question of Sport debuts on BBC1.

Paul McCartney publicly announces that he has left The Beatles, and the music world is shocked to hear the 'fab four' are disbanding.

Agatha Christie's thriller Passenger to Frankfurt is published as is Germaine Greer's book The Female Eunuch.

BBC Radio 4 first broadcasts consumer affairs magazine programme You and Yours and the first Thought for the Day. Both will still be running fifty years later.

Drug and alcohol abuse is rife among music artists. Jimi Hendrix is rushed to a London hospital in September where he died of an overdose of barbiturates and alcohol. After his death, the re-released Voodoo Chile by the Jimi Hendrix Experience reaches number 1 in the charts.

Simon and Garfunkel's Bridge Over Troubled Water, Smokey Robinson and The Miracles Tears of a Clown and Dave Edmunds, I Hear You Knockin' all reach No 1 in the charts.

In June, actor Laurence Olivier becomes the first actor to be made a Lord when he is made a life peer in the Queen's Birthday Honours list. Born in 1907 to a non-theatrical family, his father, a clergyman, decided Laurence should become an actor. He attended drama school in London and had his first West End success in Noël Coward's Private Lives in 1930.

The first Glastonbury Festival is held, known as the Pilton Pop, Folk and Blues Festival at Worthy Farm, with only 1,500 attendees. Admission was £1, which included free camping and a pint of milk.

Carry on up the Jungle, The Railway Children and Wuthering Heights based on the classic Emily Brontë novel of the same name are all released at the cinema.

The half-crown coin ceases to be legal tender. The British half crown was a denomination of sterling coinage worth 1/8 of one pound, or two shillings and six pence. It was first issued in 1549, in the reign of Edward VI but not displaying its value on the reverse until 1893. No half-crowns were issued in the reign of Mary, but from the reign of Elizabeth I half-crowns were issued in every reign except that of Edward VIII.

1976 The Year

1976 was a year of unease in many areas. The situation in Ireland deteriorated, with killings on both sides, and Direct Rule was imposed on Northern Ireland in March. We were involved in 'The 3rd Cod War' disputing North Atlantic fishing rights, but later conceded to Iceland's increased fishing limits, resulting in a blow to our fishing industry from which it never really recovered. The weather swung between hurricane winds in January, to a record-breaking heatwave in June, followed by drought and compulsory standpipes in many areas for daily water supplies.

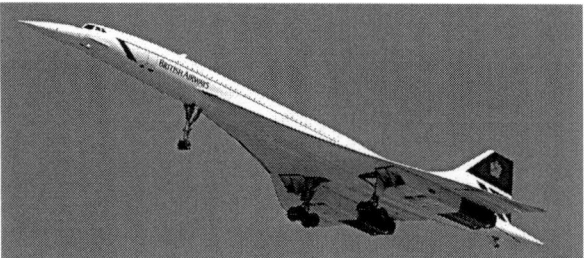

Concorde made its first commercial flight, and Body Shop opened its first store in Brighton. Britain won the Eurovision Song Contest with 'Save Your Kisses For Me' sung by Brotherhood Of Man in April, but August saw over 60 people injured in rioting at the Notting Hill Carnival.

In August, the iconic clock 'Big Ben' towering over The Houses of Parliament broke down when the chiming mechanism failed after more than 100 years of use. The clock was shut down for nine months, the longest break in operation since its completion in 1859, during which time, the "Pips" were broadcast by BBC Radio 4.

Eleven In 1976

For most eleven-year-olds in 1976 the 11+ selective exam was almost totally phased out and comprehensive schools were the norm. It was the start of growing up but at home there was still plenty of fun.

Chopper bikes were a status symbol; space hoppers were still 'cool' and there were video games and colour TV. The BBC introduced Paddington Bear and Kermit the Frog brought in the Muppet Show.

How Much Did It Cost?

The Average Pay:	£3,380 (£65 p.w)
The Average House:	£12,000
Loaf of White Bread:	19p
Pint of Milk:	9p
Pint of Beer:	33p
Gallon of Petrol:	77p (17p/litre)
12mnths Road Tax	£48
Newspapers:	7p
To post a letter in UK:	8½p
TV Licence	£8 Black & White £18 Colour

YOU WERE ELEVEN

Popular Culture

Charles, the then Prince of Wales, opens Brent Cross Shopping Centre in London. This is the UK's first out-of-town American style indoor shopping centre, whilst Body Shop founder, Anita Roddick, opens a little green shop in Brighton, the first branch in the retail chain for skin care products and cosmetics. Roddick had a belief that business could *'be a force for good'* saying years later, *"We've never been your average cosmetics company, always campaigning, change-making and smashing beauty industry standards"*.

Abba tops the charts with Mamma Mia and Fernando and Brotherhood of Man win the 21st Eurovision Song Contest, representing the UK with their song Save Your Kisses for Me and keep the top spot in the UK chart.

The Damned release New Rose, the first single marketed as "punk rock" and Elton John and Kiki Dee have the number one hit Don't Go Breaking My Heart, a first No 1 for both artists, staying at the top for six weeks, and a surprise No 1 came for The Wurzels with The Combine Harvester.

BBC television has a host of new shows this year; Paddington, based on the books by Michael Bond; Ronnie Barker and David Jason star in the comedy series Open All Hours; the US series Starsky & Hutch brought David Soul and Paul Michael Glaser into our living rooms.

ITV also rivalled the BBC for hit shows, The Muppet Show, George and Mildred, The Fall and Rise of Reginald Perrin and The Bionic Woman amongst them.

The Royal National Theatre, founded by Laurence Olivier in 1963 and hitherto based at The Old Vic in Waterloo, relocates and opens on the South Bank in London, and The Royal Shakespeare Company stages Macbeth in Stratford-upon-Avon, with Ian McKellen and Judi Dench.

1981 The Year

In 1981 Margaret Thatcher's conservative government has been in power for two years. The UK had entered a recession with rising unemployment and the government introduced policies to push privatisation of state-owned industries and utilities and the reform of the trade unions. Teenagers enjoyed reading magazines like Smash Hits, while music, fashion, and pop culture played a significant role in shaping their experiences.

Charles, Prince of Wales, marries Lady Diana Spencer and more than 30 million viewers watch on television – the second highest TV audience of all time in Britain. The Yorkshire Ripper is arrested; the Brixton Riots erupted, and the first London Marathon takes place with 7,500 runners participating.

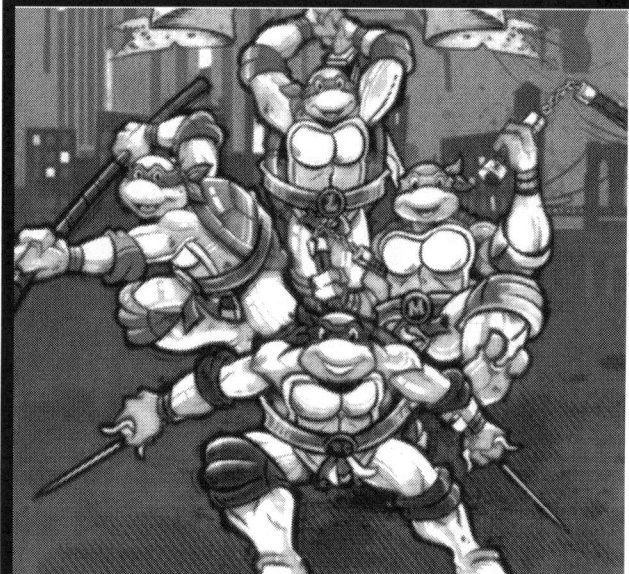

Times Are Changing

In 1981, young people were experiencing unprecedented freedoms; with new and exciting designs and creativity in both fashion, and entertainment for the "baby boomers" who had come of age. Music had a huge influence on the 80's decade, MTV launched showing music videos of tracks dominating Top of the Pops.

Ghetto Blasters and Walkman's blared out tunes, and toys included Mattel's Barbie dolls and Palitoy's Action Men. Techno toys, like Simon Says and Nintendo games consoles became popular, and we fell in love with Teenage mutant ninja turtles who lived underground.

Life at Sixteen

Sixteen in 1981, you could leave school; join the army; legally buy cigarettes as well as smoke them; pubs were only open lunchtimes and evenings, and you couldn't have a beer unless an "adult" over 18 bought it for you and you were eating a meal.

Girls went crazy over Princess Diana's 'shaggy bob' hairstyle, and fashion was soft 'New Romantic' and carrying on the trend for sportswear, girls increasingly wore stylish gym wear in their day-to-day life.

How Much Did It Cost?

The Average Pay	£7,350 (£141 p.w.)
The Average House	£23.730
Loaf of White Bread	36p
Pint of Milk	18p
Pint of Beer	51p
Gallon of Petrol	£1.60 (35p/litre)
Newspapers	12p-15p
To Post a Letter in UK	14p
12 Mths Road Tax	£70
TV Licence	£46

You Were Sixteen

Popular Culture

BBC Two's The Hitchhiker's Guide to the Galaxy television adaptation begins airing; it subsequently receives a Royal Television Society award as 'Most Original Programme' of the year. BBC1 begins showing the American cartoon series Scooby-Doo whilst ITV shows the pilot episode of Magnum P.I. starring Tom Selleck. Ken Barlow marries Deirdre Langton on Coronation Street and when ITV broadcasts the supernatural, horror, film, **The Omen**, they receive hundreds of complaints the following morning, of viewers being horrified.

John Lennon, shot and killed in December 1980, is top of the charts in January with **Imagine** and again in February with **Woman**. Bucks Fizz win the Eurovision Song Contest with the song **Making Your Mind Up**. They represented the United Kingdom and go to the top of the charts.

Academy Award-winning film **Chariots of Fire** and **For Your Eyes Only**, the twelfth James Bond film starring Roger Moore as James Bond, are released in cinemas and Andrew Lloyd Webber debuts his musical **Cats**.

The first book In the **Little Miss** series Little Miss Bossy, (the female counterpart to the Mr. Men series) is first published.

Queen releases their **Greatest Hits** compilation album which becomes the all-time best-selling album in the United Kingdom; Adam and the Ants secured the record for most top 10 hits in 1981 with six hit singles including **Stand and Deliver** and **Prince Charming** which both went to No 1 and the best-selling, and Christmas No 1 went to The Human League and **Don't You Want Me.**

1986 The Year

In 1986 Margaret Thatcher's conservative government is in power. Deregulation in the financial markets known as the 'Big Bang' transformed the City of London and paved the way for modern financial practices. Unemployment reached a postwar high, affecting 14.4% of the workforce.

The Pet Shop Boys & Madonna featured in the singles chart and women's fashion trends include the iconic shoulder pads, power suits, and neon lycra. Sub-zero temperatures hit the country and there are heavy snowfalls in February; journalist John McCarthy is kidnapped in Beirut; The Oprah Winfrey Show has its national debut and Mad Cow disease was first found in UK cattle.

The Soviet Nuclear reactor at Chernobyl explodes releasing radioactive material across much of Europe; the Space Shuttle Challenger disintegrates after launching, killing all seven astronauts on board and Comet Halley reaches the closest point to the Earth.

The Chernobyl nuclear reactor after the explosion

When You Were 21

Twenty-one in 1986, you were enjoying the 1980's fitness craze. Celebrities made aerobics videos; Health Clubs and Gyms, predominantly for men, became the place to be and to be seen whilst women exercised in the privacy of their own home, to a well-worn VHS copy of 'Jane Fonda's Workout', or to Diana Moran 'The Green Goddess', who appeared on TV screens wearing her trade-mark green leotard telling millions of BBC Breakfast viewers to 'wake up and shape up' with her aerobics routines.

How Much Did It Cost?

The Average Pay:	£8,955 (£172 pw)
The Average House:	£48,000
Loaf of White Bread:	43p
Pint of Milk:	19p
Pint of Beer:	82p
Gallon of Petrol:	£1.79 (40p/litre)
12mnths Road Tax	£100
Newspapers:	18-23p
To post a letter in UK:	17p
TV Licence	£58 Colour

You Were 21

Popular Culture

In the now-infamous May episode of Dallas, the prime-time CBS soap resurrected the character, Bobby Ewing, who had been killed off at the end of the prior season. Bobby comes out of the shower and the whole of the 1985/1986 season is explained as a lengthy dream of his wife, Pamela Barnes – it didn't happen!

Music had a huge influence on the 80's decade, **MTV** showed music videos of tracks dominating **Top of the Pops**. **Ghetto Blasters** and **Walkman's** blasted out tunes. The best-selling single of the year was **Don't Leave Me This Way** by The Communards.

Toys included **Barbie Dolls** and **Action Men**. Techno toys, like **Simon Says** and **Nintendo** games consoles became popular, **Transformers** became the Toy of the Year and **Trivial Pursuit** wins 'Game of the Year'.

Television had a huge number of new releases including **Catchphrase** the game show with the computer-generated character **Mr. Chips**; **Lovejoy**; the contemporary comedy **Bread**; **Beadle's About** and the hugely popular **Casualty**. Whilst from Australia came the hit soap opera **Neighbours**.

The Sun Always Shines on T.V. by A-ha reached No 1 in the charts as did **When the Going Gets Tough, the Tough Get Going** by Billy Ocean; Cliff Richard's **Living Doll** featuring the cast of the television series **The Young Ones**; Spitting Image's **The Chicken Song**; **The Edge of Heaven** by Wham!

The cinema entertained, thrilled and frightened us with **Rocky IV**, **Back to the Future**, **Out of Africa**, **Down and Out in Beverly Hills** and **Aliens**.

1965

SPORTING HEADLINES

MARCH The Grand National at Aintree Racecourse is won by Jay Trump ridden by American amateur jockey Tommy Smith. The favourite, Freddie, came a close second.

The Cheltenham Gold Cup is won by Arkle, bought in 1960 for 1,150 guineas by the Duchess of Westminster and named Arkle after a mountain overlooking her Scottish estate

The 1965 Five Nations Championship was the thirty-sixth in the series. Ten matches were played between 9 January and 27 March. It was contested by England, France, Ireland, Scotland and Wales. Wales missed out on a fourth Grand Slam after losing to France at Stade Colombes despite winning the overall title.

Arkle the Cheltenham Gold Cup Champion

APRIL At the Masters in Atlanta, Jack Nicklaus, nicknamed 'The Golden Bear', shoots a record 17 under par with a score of 271 (at the time a record), to win the tournament. At age 25 this was the second of his six Masters titles.

MAY In the final match of the FA Cup Final at Wembley Stadium, Liverpool beats Leeds United 2-1. The crowd of 100,000 watched the match which was goalless on both sides for the first 90 minutes.

JULY For the second consecutive year in an all-Australian final, Roy Emerson successfully defends his title and defeats Fred Stolle to retain the Wimbledon Men's Singles Championship.

Jack Nicklaus wins the Masters

Margaret Smith Court (AUS) defeated the defending champion Maria Bueno (BRA) to win the Women's Singles Championship.

OCTOBER Jim Clark wins the 19th World Championship Formula One season over ten races, in a Lotus-Climax. It was his second and last championship.

Jim Clark, winner of the 1965 F1 Championship

SPORTING EVENTS

MUHAMMAD ALI Vs. SONNY LISTON 25th MAY 1965

THE GREATEST

On 25th May 1965 in Lewiston, Maine, Cassius Marcellus Clay nicknamed the 'Louisville Lip,' (who went on to be known as Muhammad Ali) beat Sonny Liston nicknamed 'Big Bear' for boxing's World Heavyweight Championship. Clay won with a first-round knockout. A botched count by the referee and the infamous "phantom punch", have been subject to debate of a fix ever since. Lasting less than one full round, Clay knocked out Liston at the 1:44 mark. This was a shocking result with hardly anyone seeing the punch that took him down. This was the second win of two fights between Clay and Liston, the first in 1964 and both fights are among the most controversial fights in the sport's history. Clay a legendary boxer and cultural icon had mesmerising agility in the ring, he was known to say he would "Float like a butterfly, sting like a bee" as he would glide around his opponents, light on his feet, and then suddenly strike with the force of a bee's sting.

Cassius Marcellus Clay Jr. was born in Louisville, Kentucky in 1942 and started boxing when he was 12. Having won over 100 bouts in amateur competitions, he then won the 'International Golden Gloves' heavyweight title in 1959 and was entered into the Olympic Games in Rome in 1960, where he won a heavyweight Gold Medal. Clay turned professional and won his first 19 bouts which then gave him the right to challenge Sonny Liston for the World Heavyweight title. Not long after he won this world title, Cassius Clay was at a gathering with his friend Malcolm X, the leader of the African American Muslim group known as the 'Nation of Islam' and a few days later, he announced he was joining the organisation. A descendant of formerly enslaved ancestors, he rejected his family name – given by the slave owners – and took the Muslim name of Muhammad Ali.

1965

A REMBRANDT RUMPUS

A portrait of 'The Artist Rembrandt Van Rijn's Son' Titus' was sold at Christie's, Auction House, London in March 1965. Prior to an auction it was customary for buyers to choose their own 'signals' for the auctioneer. American collector Norton Simon had a complicated array of instructions; if he was sitting, he was bidding, if he stood up, he had stopped bidding; if he sat down again, he would raise his finger to indicate that he was resuming bidding.

The auctioneer eventually brought down the hammer at 700,000 guineas, having missed a later bid from Simon. The bidding was forced to reopen, and Simon took ownership of the painting at the closing value of 760,000 guineas (£798,000). The auctioneer Peter Chance said this was *"the worst moment"* of his working life.

THE 'F' WORD

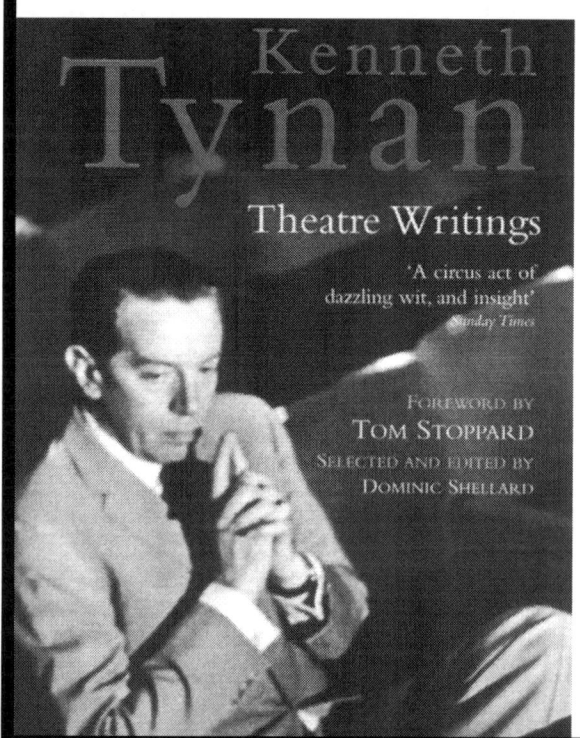

English theatre critic and writer Kenneth Peacock Tynan was possibly the first person to, intentionally, say the four-letter word "f***" on British television. Initially he was a critic at The Observer where his opinions, then deemed outrageous, were very much against theatre censorship. While appearing live on the BBC, Tynan used the word as a synonym for sexual intercourse while discussing whether sex acts should be shown on TV and film.

There was an immediate outcry with hundreds of members of the public complaining to the BBC. One concerned citizen wrote to Queen Elizabeth II and also suggested Tynan *"ought to have his bottom smacked."* Two weeks later, Mary Whitehouse founded The National Viewers' and Listeners' Association. Following a shamed apology from the BBC, profanity was unacceptable on TV broadcast networks for another few decades.

CULTURAL EVENTS

DUKE OF YORK'S FIRST LESBIAN CAPER

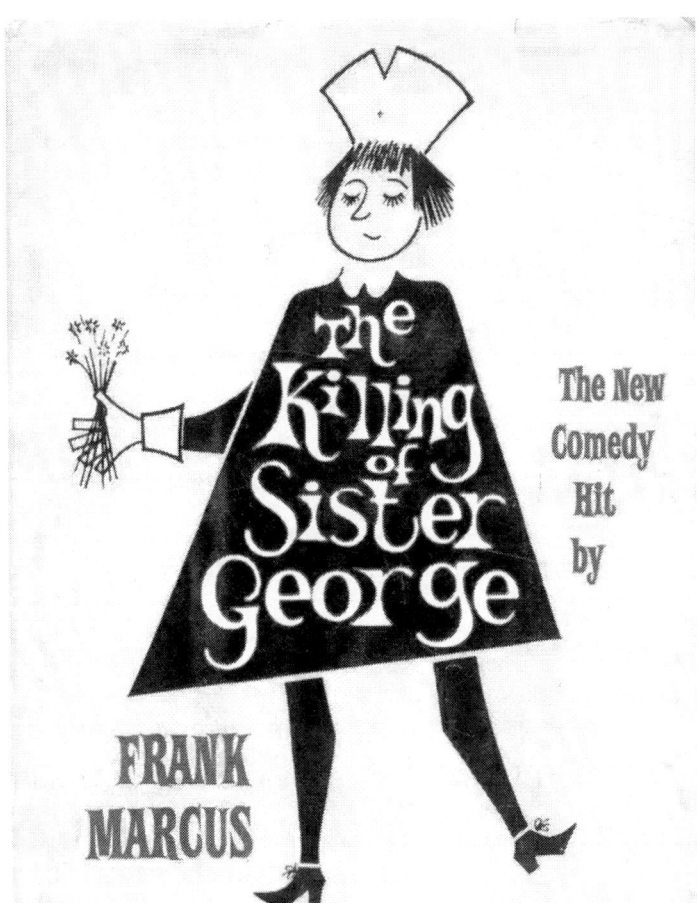

Following a preview at the Bristol Old Vic, The Killing of Sister George a Frank Marcus' farce premiered in London at the Duke of York's Theatre. This was one of the first mainstream British plays with lesbian characters.

Sister George is a beloved character in the popular radio series Applehurst. The character is a district nurse who tends to the medical needs and personal problems of the local villagers. The 'real-life' character June Buckridge, (played by Beryl Reid) is a slightly sadistic masculine woman, the opposite of the sweet character she plays.

Often known as George, she lives with Alice "Childie" McNaught, a younger, dim-witted woman, whom she often verbally and, sometimes physically, abuses. When George discovers that her character is to be killed off on the radio, she becomes impossible to work and live with.

HELP! IT'S THE BEATLES

British musical comedy-adventure film Help! directed by Richard Lester, starring The Beatles had its Royal World Premiere at the London Pavilion Theatre.

The main events include the group struggling to protect Ringo Starr from a sinister eastern cult and a pair of mad scientists, who are obsessed with obtaining a sacrificial ring sent to him by a fan. The soundtrack Help! was released in August as the band's fifth studio album.

Seven of the fourteen songs appeared in the film and the album topped the charts in the UK, Australia, Germany and America, and received flattering reviews.

1965

THE SWEETEST WAY

One of the most important inventions of the decade was Aspartame, an artificial non-saccharide sweetener, 200 times sweeter than sucrose. It was invented in 1965 by James M. Schlatter, a chemist working for Searle a pharmaceutical company in the US.

He discovered aspartame while trying to create a cure for stomach ulcers, but when he licked his fingers to pick up a piece of paper, he noticed a very sweet taste. He found that aspartame could be used as an artificial sweetener, which could help people avoid ingesting too much sugar in their diet. Aspartame went on to become the most popular artificial sweetener in the world and is now used in many products including soft drinks, chewing gum, tabletop sweeteners, and diet foods like yogurt and sauces.

THE VALPARAISO EARTHQUAKE

A powerful 90-second earthquake registering between 6.5 and 7.5 on the Richter scale struck the Santiago, Valparaiso, and Coquimbo provinces of central Chile on 28th March. At the mining location El Cobre, the earthquake sent a landslide into a dam and the flood and mud buried hundreds of residents.
Although the epicentre was about 80 miles north of the Chilean capital of Santiago, the quake was felt throughout the country and as far away as Buenos Aires, about 700 miles distant. The earthquake struck at 12.33pm on a Sunday when many Chileans had just finished preparing their lunch or had just returned from church services. 400-500 people were killed, over 21,000 houses collapsed and 70,000 had to be repaired. The country lies in the 'Ring of Fire' an area where many of the worlds active volcanoes and seismic activities are concentrated.

Science And Nature

Touch Screen Technology

At the Royal Radar Establishment in Malvern, United Kingdom, Eric Arthur Johnson invented the first finger-driven touchscreen and filed his first patent application in August 1965. Johnson's invention was a radar screen used by air traffic controllers in the UK and remained in use until the late 1990s. The capacitive touchscreen is like the technology used in modern smartphones.

This type of touchscreen panel uses an insulator, like glass, that is coated with a transparent conductor such as indium tin oxide (ITO). The "conductive" part is usually a human finger, which makes for a fine electrical conductor. Johnson also foresaw that the design could work as a keyboard for entering characters. The initial technology could only process one touch at a time, unlike the modern day "multitouch" which was still some years away.

The Mariner 4 Mission To Mars

Mariner 4, the second of two Mars flyby attempts, was the first spacecraft to obtain and transmit close range images of Mars. After its launch in November 1964 and a journey of hundreds of millions of kilometres, Mariner 4 passed within 9844 kilometres of Mars on July 14, 1965.

Designed for planetary exploration without landing, the spacecraft was used to conduct closeup scientific observations of Mars and to transmit these observations back to Earth.

The close-up pictures first seen of the Martian surface revealed a cratered and moon-like surface, contrary to previous, even conservative, estimates of the Martian topography and life on Mars. Initially Mariner 4 was to remain in space for eight months, but the mission lasted about three years in solar orbit.

Mariner 4 and photos of craters on Mars

1965 LIFESTYLES OF

1965 was a year to be young. In these 'swinging sixties', the baby boomer generation was coming of age and youth culture was flourishing, with post-war austerity finally having given way to a decade of optimism. Rock music was in full swing, and people were crazy about The Beatles, The Rolling Stones, The Kinks and The Who. Pink Floyd formed, helping build a growing psychedelic rock movement.

The spotlight was on fashion too, and Mary Quant led the way with simple, colourful designs and of course, the mini-skirt, which shocked and delighted in equal measure. This post-war generation was the first to have money to buy records, makeup and new clothes and there were dozens of new styles being invented every day.

But, Britain was still a country in which older men wore hats and carried umbrellas; few people had a telephone, and thousands of working-class families still had outside toilets.

As a child you could spend your pocket money, probably still about 6d (2p) a week, on your favourite sweet treats. Rolls of Love Hearts were put in their special Christmas Crackers by Swizzels. They were such a success that the fizzy sweets with their fun messages became permanent, selling at 3d (1p) a pack.

One of the best sweets for sharing were Rowntree's Fruit Gums. Their famous slogan: "Don't forget the Fruit Gums, Mum" was changed to "Chum", not "Mum" in 1961 when the company became aware of accusations of 'pester power' and didn't want the nation's mothers disapproving of them as a brand.

Treets, Peanut, Toffee or Chocolate, which 'Melt in your mouth, not in your hand', and more and more sweets in packets rather than being weighed out by the shopkeeper from jars and handed over in little paper bags

EVERYDAY PEOPLE

Your holiday during the sixweek summer break was likely to be in Britain. Holiday camps such as Butlins with their 'Red Coats' offered hours of fun, coaches could take you to the seaside and owning a caravan was becoming popular too.

In 1965 the nuclear family was still the norm, father out at work and mother busy with the housework which was time consuming before the general possession of electrical labour-saving devices. Washing up was done by hand and laundry gradually moved to machines over the decade. Twin tubs, one for washing and one for spinning, became popular in the late 60's and were usually wheeled into the kitchen to be attached to the cold tap and afterwards, have the waste-water emptied into the sink. The 'housewife' had to be at home to transfer the wet washing from the washing tub to the spinning tub.

Goods came to you. The milkman delivered the milk to your doorstep, the baker brought the baskets of bread to the door, the greengrocer delivered and the 'pop man' came once a week with 'dandelion and burdock', 'cherryade' or 'cream soda' and the rag and bone man visited the street for your recycling.

January 1st – 7th 1965

IN THE NEWS

Friday 1 — **"A Happy New Year"** It was a happy new year for Britain's *'King of Soccer'*, soon to be *Sir* Stanley Matthews, after being named on Prime Minister Harold Wilson's first honours list.

Saturday 2 — **"A Dearer Sweet Treat"** *'Adjustments'* made to cinema ticket prices across Britain, raised the cost of a seat by 6d. To make matters worse, Cadbury's Chocolate, often a companion to a good film, announced price increases of Dairy Milk, Bourneville and Milk Tray due to a shortage of raw materials.

Sunday 3 — **"Roll-On Ships"** The Ministry of Transport has commissioned a new type of ship, capable of on-and-off loading without the use of cranes, for the transport of heavy engineering loads in shallow waters. The demand for the vessel comes from the increasing weight of industrial components.

Monday 4 — **"Docker Shortage"** 33-large vessels lay idle in Merseyside Ports due to a shortage of dockers, with a further 29 operating undermanned. 3,315 men stayed home causing the build-up of 150 ships in the port.

Tuesday 5 — **"Come to Scotland"** A new £30,000 per year publicity stunt designed to drive new Scottish business and industry, has launched, aiming to show people throughout Britain, including residents of Scotland, the benefits of living and working in their country.

Wednesday 6 — **"Supersonic Defence"** With the arrival of the RAF's new Lightning Mark Three aircraft, Britain is now able to provide supersonic air support for the defence of Malaysia against impending Indonesian invasion; the planes can fly non-stop from England to Singapore.

Thursday 7 — **"The Kray Brothers"** Twin brothers, Ronald and Reginald Kray, have been arrested and charged with making menaces by force, demanding money with the intent to steal.

HERE IN BRITAIN

"Never Marry a Cleric"

The latest issue of the Anglican monthly 'Prism' features a piece by Mrs Brenda Wolfe, wife to a Parish Priest in Wigan, on the *'lousy job'* of being a parson's wife. The problem of *'always being second-best'* to her husband was the topic of her article, and she wrote of her youthful ambition when she married, that has since become like *'being the favoured mistress of a married man'*.

She has raised their children practically on her own, with her husband always on duty. She dare not even *'twist'* at a Parish dance lest she might cause comment.

AROUND THE WORLD

"Bird-Song Whistles"

Citroen has found a link between bird song and cars. As part of a new year's publicity stunt, French motorists have been gifted a set of implements from which they can create characteristic notes of many birds including, thrush, black-birds, tawny owls and cuckoos; some involving more complicated instructions than others.

To mimic the red-legged partridge, one must hold the whistle in the palm of their hand, before *'blowing out pronouncing cacz, cacz.'* The bizarre stunt is meant to lure people away from the highways, instead encouraging time in woodlands.

Unsung Heros Of The Seas

A report published earlier this month by the RNLI records details of the 443 lives saved, and 71 inshore boats rescued, during 1964 - the most of any year on record. The service had more call-outs last year than any since the organisation's inception in 1824. Perhaps because lifeboatmen are characteristically unostentatious about their work, perhaps because the service they perform makes no financial demands on the ratepayer or taxpayer, many people seem unaware of the hundreds of lives they save and the risks and discomfort they undergo. The lifeboat is expected to be on hand when needed, like police cars, fire engines or ambulances. That the Royal National Life-boat Institution is supported entirely by voluntary subscriptions probably only occurs to the average person for a few moments a year when he sees a collection box or a poster appealing for funds.

Yet in coastal towns and villages the threat of disaster at sea is more imminent, the lifeboat service is more familiar and volunteers to man the boats continue to come forward amidst the changing nature of the services they have been called on to perform in recent years. The decline of the fishing industry in many parts of the country has been accompanied by a phenomenal increase in the number of pleasure-boat owners, out in force during the main holiday months of July, August and September.

As an official put it, the institution's charter is to rescue people from the sea without distinction between nationalities or circumstances and this includes *'bloody fools'* as much as those who are victims of an Act of God. A glance at the accounts of rescues in the institution's quarterly journal will convince both the unfortunate and the foolish how great is their debt to those who uncomplainingly risk their lives to save others.

January 8th – 14th 1965

IN THE NEWS

Friday 8   **"Fog-Signs"** The Minister for Transport has approved temporary 'fog-signs' on the motorway to be placed at strategic positions to warn motorists of localised, patches of poor visibility. The sign will show the word FOG surrounded by a red triangle.

Saturday 9   **"Faith in the System"** British pop singer, Adam Faith, has been arrested in South Africa whilst attempting to leave the country. Mr Faith refused to perform many of his contracted shows protesting at the government's prohibition of mixed-race audiences.

Sunday 10   **"NHS In Danger"** Following a six and a half hour meeting of the Council of Medical Practitioners Union, a statement was released warning that unless working and wage conditions improve, the NHS is at risk of collapse.

Monday 11   **"The Witness-List Goes On"** 667 witnesses are to be called in a £143,000 embezzlement trial at the Edinburgh High Court. Highland and Lowland Hatcheries Ltd have been accused of embezzling money given for the sale, housing and feeding of sows.

Tuesday 12   **"Fair Fares"** British Rail, after lowering peak railway ticket prices by a third to attract more rail users, has announced the re-raising of prices. The reduction did not attract enough extra revenue to be sustainable.

Wednesday 13   **"Fresh Sea Beer"** Beer barrels were amongst the cargo washed up on British shores following a night of intense storms in the English Channel and the western approaches. The wind reached speeds of over 85 mph causing havoc for vessels.

Thursday 14   **"Ireland Meets"** For the first time since the assimilation of Northern Ireland into the UK, the Prime Ministers of the state and the Republic of Ireland met in Belfast. Many hope that this may forge the path for a friendly and cooperative relationship.

HERE IN BRITAIN

"More Time for Sleep"

A study by Liverpool University has concluded that retirement both allows for *'more time to sleep'*, but also an ineptitude to grasp modern technological developments, like the use of a telephone. The study, looking at over 1,000 retired men, found that many elderly people had never used a telephone, and would not even be able to in an emergency. Costing around £1,000, and expected to take 18 months, the investigation hopes to *'establish the difference between men who find retirement a door for opportunity … and those who lapse into inactivity.*

AROUND THE WORLD

"Star of India"

Nine of 23 valuable gems, including the 563-carat sapphire known as the Star of India, have been recovered by the New York Police from a locker at a bus terminal in Miami, Florida.

The stones were stolen from the American Museum of Natural History in October last year but now found following an anonymous tip via telephone hundreds of miles from where they were last seen. Contained within a damp canvas bag, it appears that the precious gems were kept buried in sand or sea for a long period of time.

The 'Met' Office

For 42 years the Meteorological Office has been broadcasting weather forecasts to the masses. Reports of temperatures *'on the Air Ministry roof'*, the home of the Met Office broadcasting studio, have filled the ears of Londoners almost daily, making it one of the best-known spots in the whole city. Something of an anticlimax, the readings were never actually taken from the roof of the Air Ministry itself, instead from a building owned by the department in Kingsway and, following the merging of the Air Ministry with the Ministry of Defence last year, the phrase was replaced by *'the roof of the London Weather Centre'*.

In fact, the roof of the actual recordings has since changed from Kingsway too. The rapid growth in height and stature of the London skyline has meant that Met Office rooftop sites are becoming ever more shadowed and the State House, a 15-storey building, towering 175ft high, just across the road from the Weather Centre, is now the new home of British forecasts. 50 staff work throughout the day and night to provide up-to-date forecasts to be distributed across the country, to the Post Office, for their telephone weather service; to electricity and gas boards, for the planning of power demand; to clients in commerce and industry and to building firms and to transport services.

Created in 1855, the Meteorological Department of the Board of Trade was created for the benefit of shipping. As equipment and forecasting techniques became more reliable weather reports by the BBC became available to the public from 1922. Attached to the Air Ministry amidst the growing needs of aviation, the international prominence of the Met Office was such that the director was made the First president of the World Meteorological Organization in 1950.

January 15th – 21st 1965

IN THE NEWS

Friday 15 — **"Slipping into Deeper Sleep"** In a statement by his physicians, it was announced to the world that Sir Winston Churchill is *'slipping into a deeper sleep'* following a cerebral thrombosis. The Queen has asked to be kept informed.

Saturday 16 — **"Far East Support"** The Government has announced a further 1,000 troops are to be sent to Far East Command in Singapore to *'facilitate the rotation of specialist troops'* between operational and other areas across the region.

Sunday 17 — **"Record Loading"** Dockers working at Ellesmere Port in Cheshire have broken a record by loading 1,160 tons of caustic soda onto a ship in eight-and-a-half hours. They loaded the cargo at a rate of 136 tons per hour.

Monday 18 — **"Tobacco Ban"** The Board of Trade has warned tobacco suppliers that, should Rhodesia take unilateral independence, the British Government would place a ban on tobacco imports from the country.

Tuesday 19 — **"Pirate Hunting"** In conjunction with other European States, the UK are to sign a convention outlawing pirate radio stations; however, the possibility that the Isle of Man might refuse could mean that pirate ships continue operations in UK waters.

Wednesday 20 — **"Canal Closure"** Manchester ship canal was closed for over 17 hours after a ship discharged 8,000 gallons of petrol into the water. The crew of the S.S. Brodick tried to hose as much as possible of the affected water towards the shore.

Thursday 21 — **"A Dead Duchess"** A coffin found on a building site in Stepney has been confirmed to contain Ann Mowbray, Duchess of York, the child bride of Richard Duke of York, one of the princes believed to have been murdered in the Tower of London in 1483.

HERE IN BRITAIN

"India By Luxury Sleeper Coach"

The newest offering to the British traveller was launched outside the Savoy Hotel by its creator, Sir Henry Lunn. The 'Mobilotel', a 36-seater and sleeper coach will tour rural parts of India, Pakistan and Asia-Minor, places where hotel accommodation is below par.

At night, the crew wind a handle, extending the sides of the vehicle, turning it into a comfortable and spacious dormitory; men to the left, women to the right, couples in the middle. Air conditioning and power for the on-board kitchen, to hopefully avoid stomach upsets, is supplied from a generator set up outside.

AROUND THE WORLD

"Skilled Britons Wanted"

Representatives from Queensland, Australia, arrived in London to recruit several hundred skilled British workers to emigrate to their State.. Enquiries have come in from 300 people across London and Southampton, as the three-man-mission prepares to embark on a 10-week tour of British industrial centres.

Although the workers have been assured high wages, the representatives have said that *'we cannot promise a pie in the sky'*. What they did confirm is that immigrants would have space shared with just one and a half people per square mile, compared with the 570 in London.

THE MONTE CARLO RALLY

For the second successive year Britain has carried off the top prize in international rallying with an outright victory in the 34th Monte Carlo Rally. The winning 1275cc Mini Cooper S was driven to victory by 26-year-old Finn Timo Makinen, with Buckinghamshire-born mechanic Paul Easter as co-driver. Makinen and Easter stormed to a 500-point lead over second place, Germany's Eugen Bohringer and his Porshe 904; eight other British cars featured in the top 20, making it one of the most successful ever rallies for British engineering.

Makinen attributed his incredible lead to *'Scandinavian technique'*, going on record to say that it would take many years for a British driver to master the necessary skills to drive the Mini across what were some of the worst snow and Ice conditions to ever plague the course. Nevertheless, the triumph will do wonders for the British Motor Corporation. The win was the second for Mini, who had their first taste of success just last year with Paddy Hopkirk, and also coincides with the building of the one-millionth Mini Cooper at their factory in Birmingham.

A particular highlight from this year's race saw the final spot on the podium go to Mrs. Pat Moss-Carlson in her Swedish works-Saab. This is the highest ever finishing position for a female driver in the rally, awarding her the Coup de Dames for the fifth year. Despite a strong performance from the British, it was the Swedish who took home the overall team prize. Of the 238 starters, spread across London, Paris, Monaco, Athens, Lisbon, Frankfurt, Minsk and Warsaw, just 35 completed the road stage; a further 11 were knocked out during the mountain tests, including a Citroen that plunged over a 30ft drop; the driver was quickly taken to hospital with broken ribs.

January 22nd – 28th 1965

Friday 22 — **"18 More Miles"** In melting snow and a wintry breeze, the Minister for Transport opened the newest section of the M1, an 18-mile extension up to Leicester. The link will cut the journey time between the city and London by a fifth.

Saturday 23 — **"Fish Bandits"** Salmon poachers, whose weapons of choice include poison and dynamite for their illegal hauls, are to face much harsher penalties in England and Wales. The change comes following complaints by fisherman of the damage done to salmon and trout rivers. Poachers can catch around £500 worth of fish every night.

Sunday 24 — **"Death of Sir Winston"** Former wartime Prime Minister, Sir Winston Churchill, died *'in peace and without pain'* at his London home in the presence of his wife and three children.

Monday 25 — **"New Cardinals"** The Pope has announced 27 new Cardinals, bringing the total number to an unprecedented 103. Among them are both the Archbishop of Westminster and the Archbishop of Armagh.

Tuesday 26 — **"Sent Off (to Prison)"** 10 professional, and former professional, footballers have been found guilty of match fixing, with all of them sentenced to imprisonment and fined £5,000. James Gauld, former Mansfield Town inside forward, was deemed the perpetrator, and sentenced to four years.

Wednesday 27 — **"National Hero"** Ahead of Sir Winston Churchill's state funeral, his body has been laid to rest in Westminster Abbey where, over the next three days, more than 4,000 people per hour will pass by his catafalque.

Thursday 28 — **"A Valiant Effort"** Having been grounded since the beginning of December, the entire Valiant fleet of Bomber Command is to be scrapped after multiple cases of metal fatigue revealed an aircraft structural defect.

HERE IN BRITAIN
"The Art of Shoeing"

In an industry being swept by technical revolution, bespoke shoe craftsmen are running out of willing young apprentices. Peal and Co. Ltd, a sixth-generation establishment first opened in 1791, is to close; the shop has sold shoes and boots to the late President's Roosevelt and Kennedy; made boots for cowboy Tom Mix, Fred Astaire, Charlie Chaplin, Rudolph Valentino, Cary Grant and Marilyn Monroe and sold a Sam Browne belt to General Eisenhower. Peals learnt as long ago as 1880 that America was a certain market for their refined goods, making ruthlessly 'British' sales missions there.

AROUND THE WORLD
"Oil Road"

A 700-mile winter road running deep into the Siberian basin has been opened to maintain a constant flow of supplies to many new west Siberian oil wells. A narrow track cut through a frozen, swampy pine forest is to transfer heavy machinery and prefabricated dwellings to the remote region; the journey would take 5 days under favourable conditions, and longer in temperatures exceeding -50 degrees.

Lighter goods like food and clothing are still to be delivered by air. It is expected that the oil fields will become the country's main producer within the next five years.

BURNS NIGHT

Piping in the haggis.
The INSET shows a portrait of Robbie Burns.

Robert Burns was born in Ayrshire on the west coast of Scotland in 1759, the eldest of seven children. His birthday on 25th January, has been marked for over 200 years with feasting and recitations of his works among Scots and Hibernophiles all over the world. His father was a poor and relatively unsuccessful tenant farmer, and Robert's childhood was marked by poverty and hard manual work. Educated to read and write mainly by his self-taught father, he wrote many poems and songs in Scottish dialect while working as a farm labourer. It was only later in life that his work about the themes of love and nature, was published and became very popular. Burns fathered twelve children to four different women, the last being born on the day he died, 21st July 1796.

Burns Night Suppers are held the world over, and in Scotland are more widely observed than that of its patron saint, St. Andrew, on 30th November. The suppers generally follow the same format with a welcome to the guests, and announcements, following which the 'Selkirk Grace' is recited. Then the haggis, the 'great chieftain o' the pudding-race' a traditional meat and herb pudding, is brought in on a silver tray, piped in by a bagpipe player. 'Address To a Haggis' is recited while the haggis is served with neeps and tatties, as potatoes and turnips are called, and drams of whisky. Afterwards many of his other poems will be recited and often there will be dancing. The evening finishes with the singing of the traditional song 'Auld Lang Syne' which Burns based on an older Scottish folk song. To this day it is traditionally sung to bid farewell to the old year at the stroke of midnight on Hogmanay - New Year's Eve.

Jan 29th - Feb 4th 1965

IN THE NEWS

Friday 29 — **"Cask Shortage"** Scotch whisky suppliers are concerned that a shortage of casks may affect production. At the current rate, whilst whisky output is increasing, white oak cask supplies are declining, and prices have more than doubled in the last year.

Saturday 30 — **"Funeral of a Statesman"** Statesmen and royalty were among the many guests from around the world who arrived in London for the funeral of Sir Winston Churchill.

Sunday 31 — **"British Toy Fair"** The twelfth British Toy Fair opened in Brighton with record numbers of overseas buyers. The events largest exhibitor, Mettoy Co., sold over £200,000 worth of children's typewriters to an American and AirFix Industries also had record sales.

Monday Feb 1 — **"Addis Ababa Visit"** The Queen and Duke of Edinburgh were given a joyous welcome by Ethiopians lining the streets, as they travelled inside an ornate red and gold coach through the capital city of Addis Ababa.

Tuesday 2 — **"Troublesome Teens"** The Chief Constable of Sheffield police force has blamed the sharp increase in underage drinking on 'beat groups' performing in licensed premises. 426 young people were prosecuted last year, an increase of almost 200; most cases occurred in dance halls, where live groups or 'pop' music was playing.

Wednesday 3 — **"Ford Luxury"** The new Ford Executive Zodiac, the most luxurious Ford yet, has been ergonomically perfected using the help of a computer, which ran strenuous tests that simulated over 400,000 miles of travel.

Thursday 4 — **"Online Bookings"** *"Britain's most sophisticated message processing system"* was launched by the British Overseas Airways Corporation. From now on a computer will handle the airlines world-wide teleprinter traffic in a fraction of the time of a human.

HERE IN BRITAIN

"Channel Ferry"

In the ongoing battle for cross-channel traveller business, a new car ferry between Dover and Calais has been launched. The £1.3 million Free Enterprise II can transport 200 cars and 1,200 passengers at one time and will, accompanied by her sister ship, offer round the clock travel between England and France.

During the peak holiday season, 11,500 people can make the crossing in one day. The first British-built ferry with both stern and bow opening doors contains a 13-lane vehicle bay sitting beneath fully furnished lounges, dining rooms, shops and even an arcade.

AROUND THE WORLD

"It's a Mite's World"

The United States National Science Foundation has found evidence of life over 100 miles closer to the South Pole than previously thought possible. The mite, now tentatively identified as a *Nanorchestes Antarcticus,* is described as living in *'a little world of warmth, greenery and water'* 309 miles from the South Pole.

The discovery was made by the same Hawaii based scientist who found evidence of lichen just 266 miles from the Pole, far beyond what was deemed uninhabitable. The mite has no popular name, and reportedly measures just one-hundredth of an inch long.

CHURCHILL'S FUNERAL

In what was the first state funeral for a politician in the 20th Century, thousands of people descended on London to pay tribute for the last time to the late Sir Winston Churchill, wartime Prime Minister and national hero. Millions also watched on TV, the broadcast being sent around the world. St Paul's Cathedral played host to Kings, Queens and state leaders from 112 nations. The procession contained Queen Elizabeth, the Duke of Edinburgh, the Prime Minister, and other members of the Royal Family, all of whom gave precedent to Churchill's family when leaving the ceremony.

Many could scarcely believe that 20 years had passed since the roads were filled in much the same way, but with Churchill then encouraging celebrations after leading the country to victory and out of six years of war. Though many in attendance this time would have been too young to remember, the legacy of Sir Winston transcends just the memory of those who lived through the war. *'The great maker of history',* who once said that although he loved life, he did not fear death, received a reception resembling more of a thanksgiving than a funeral and, although the country mourned, Sir Winston reaching the age of 90 was treated as an accomplishment in itself.

The military presence, including a 19-gun salute, a flypast by 16 RAF Lightning aircraft, and testimonies from his former regiments recorded the magnitude of the occasion, not least the presence of the Queen, who became the first monarch in history to attend the state funeral of a non-royal public figure. 321,000 people had walked past his catafalque over three days, creating a queue that spanned the distance between St Paul's and the Tower of London

February 5th - 11th 1965

IN THE NEWS

Friday 5 — **"Bullion Haul"** An all-night search of the Capetown Castle liner is being undertaken in the belief that the £100,000 gold bullion missing from the ship is still on board.

Saturday 6 — **"W.H. Smith's to Swindon"** W.H.Smith and Sons are to move their factory from their Lambeth Bridge site in London, to a new £2 million facility in Swindon. The 1,000 staff members have been given the opportunity to move too.

Sunday 7 — **"Phantom Fighters"** The Government is set to purchase enough US Phantom fighter jets to equip five aircraft carriers. Although the Navy has just one capable carrier, H.M.S Eagle, another, H.M.S Hermes, will be operational within two years.

Monday 8 — **"Doctor's Pay Award"** The Government, who are at risk of driving UK doctors abroad, has agreed to £5.5 million being added to NHS family doctor pay, following recommendations by the Doctors' and Dentists' Remuneration review body.

Tuesday 9 — **"Coffee Bar Hooliganism"** Legislation limiting opening hours of coffee bars and cafes has received support from 12 of 29 London boroughs. The proposal comes following an increase in youth hooliganism.

Wednesday 10 — **"Foxhunt"** One of the largest manhunts in the region took place after a police officer was shot dead in a Westmoreland village railway waiting room. Over 30 rifles and 800 rounds of ammunition were issued, with police also calling on the help of farmers. After eight hours, an armed man was apprehended.

Thursday 11 — **"Doping Scandal"** A Greyhound betting coup has been foiled after stewards cancelled a race in which one of the dogs was doped. Ladbrokes received thousands of pounds of bets on the dog, but stopped trading after realising something was wrong.

HERE IN BRITAIN

"Milking It"

Express Dairies has unveiled plans to revolutionise the milk business, with a processing method that would enable milk to be kept for months without refrigeration, even in tropical conditions.

If successful, it is estimated that Britain would be able to export as much milk as it consumes at home, increasing export revenue and also utilising seasonal gluts of milk. The process involves a refinement of high-temperature pasteurisation methods, which, although being known about for many years, have never been adapted for commercial use.

AROUND THE WORLD

"Channel Ferry"

An unprecedented six new drive-on car ferries have been announced at the unveiling of the 1,200-passenger, 150-car Valencay in St Nazaire, the first of the fleet. A joint venture between the British and French railways' service between Newhaven and Dieppe, the six vessels will provide an increase in capacity by 50% in a single year in an attempt to get ahead of the growing demand for cross-continental motoring. Advance bookings are up 17% already this year and as a result, the companies should earn their money back after just seven years.

The Wizard Of Dribble

A few days after his 50th birthday, the football league has paid tribute to Stanley Matthews. In a resolution, to be engrossed on vellum and read at the league's annual dinner in May, Matthews was spoken of as an *'example of real sportsmanship'* who has never *'at any time in the whole of his career … been guilty of any act which could have brought the game of football into disrepute.'*

In something of a bizarre coincidence, Matthews' 1953 Cup-winners medal was found on his birthday, in a safe at the Co-Operative Wholesale Society headquarters in Manchester. Matthews reportedly *'lost track'* of his most prized possession after loaning it to multiple charity events and put out an appeal to find it.

Often regarded as one of the greatest ever British football players, Stanley Matthews is still the only footballer to have been knighted whilst he was still playing professionally; winner of the inaugural Balloon D'Or, a prize given to the best European footballer, Matthews played 54 winning caps for England, and won nine British Home Championship finals. Nicknamed *The Wizard of the Dribble,* Matthews also holds the record for being the oldest person to play a game in England's premier division, the then Football League, leading Stoke City to a 3-1 victory over Fulham at age 50. At 42 years old, he also became the oldest player to represent England at international level, and was the first inductee to the English Football Hall of Fame in 2002, in honour of his contribution to the game.

Matthews never strayed far from home, playing for Stoke City in the first 19 years of his career between 1932 and 1947, before returning in 1961 for another five years following a 14-year spell with Blackpool, with whom he won the FA cup in 1953.

February 12th - 18th 1965

IN THE NEWS

Friday 12 — **"Green Belt Veto"** The Minister of Housing has vetoed a development set to house 10,000 people on the green belt at St Paul's Cray in Kent. The Minister protested on the grounds of it becoming an extension to the already sprawling London suburbia.

Saturday 13 — **"Carrier Construction"** In a clear indication of the Government's commitment to progressing with a new generation of aircraft carrier, it was announced that construction of a new ship, which is *'worth its weight in gold',* is to go ahead as scheduled.

Sunday 14 — **"Call to Quit"** 98% of doctors at a meeting of the B.M.A in Leeds voted in favour of resigning from the NHS unless their demands for better treatment and contracts were agreed to by the Government.

Monday 15 — **"Welsh TV"** 1.5 million people in Glamorgan and Monmouthshire, 600,000 of whom are Welsh speaking, have become the first people in Britain to have a choice between two independent television channels.

Tuesday 16 — **"D-Day Memorial"** The Bishop of Portsmouth has announced the extension of the Cathedral as a memorial for D-Day. The new £350,000 nave will act as a national place of commemoration this year, the 21st anniversary of the landings.

Wednesday 17 — **"Victor Allcard"** The anticipated replacement for the 25-year-old 'Alfred Robinson' ambulance boat was launched off Tower Pier. The vessel will be used to transport medical professionals to distressed boats in the Thames.

Thursday 18 — **"TSR 2"** The 'welcome back to Lancashire' ceremony planned for the supersonic TSR 2 prototype aircraft has been delayed for the third consecutive day, as bad weather continues to prohibit a test-flight and would block the view for the reporter's cameras.

HERE IN BRITAIN

"Anti-Anti-Smoking Film"

An anti-cigarette film published by the Ministry of Health had the opposite effect intended, after surveyed viewers reported feeling more convinced that the habit was safe. The research concluded that many smokers associated the cancer patients as 'suffering a rare fate of people with untypically weak lungs'; as the film reassured smokers that 'human lungs were strong and not easily damaged'. However, two out of five smokers said they would like to give up the habit if they could do so easily. Expense was the main reason, mentioned in about 50 per cent of replies.

AROUND THE WORLD

"Keeping an Eye on Things"

Engineers from Maryland have developed an optical steering system for cars and lorries that, once set on a course, can follow a road automatically. The system is the first of its kind that will not deviate from a lane, even in the event of a corner, and requires no special cables or markings in the road.

The system works via electronic memory; a scanner records the road ahead and takes notes of road lines and barriers so that, when activated, the driver can relax. Be reassured however, the driver can retake control at any time.

Valentine's Day

Victorian Valentine's Day card (left) and a 1965 card (right)

Since the end of the Second World War, Europe has seen a return to the custom of romantic and charming Valentine's Day festivities, with a rapid rise in consumerism, and American influence, in the commercialisation of the day. British love makers flock to card and chocolate shops to buy gifts for their loved ones as the country gets swept up with the air of love.

The Valentine's Day festival itself is somewhat mysterious in origin, with multiple different sources offering multiple different views. The trail goes back to the Saint Valentine, or one of three possible Saint Valentines, all of whom were martyred. The most recognised saint of the three, defied the Roman Emperor Claudius after he outlawed marriage for young men, by continuing to perform marriage ceremonies for young lovers in the street. He was beheaded for his treason. Others suggest that Saint Valentine was a Bishop also beheaded by Claudius and the third, a Valentine killed for helping Christians escape the cruelty of Roman prisons. According to one legend, an imprisoned Valentine sent the first 'Valentine greeting' to a young girl he had fallen in love with, possibly his captor's daughter, and he signed his letter *'from your Valentine'* - an expression still used to this day.

The festival itself, nevertheless, acts as a celebration of the life of Saint Valentine, possibly all three Saint Valentines, but wasn't an overtly romantic celebration until characterised as such by Geoffrey Chaucer in his 1375 poem, *'For this was sent on Seynt Valentine's day ... when every foul cometh ther to choose his mate'.* The oldest known valentine was a poem written in 1415 by Charles, Duke of Orleans, to his wife while he was imprisoned in the Tower of London following his capture at the Battle of Agincourt.

February 19th – 25th 1965

IN THE NEWS

Friday 19 — **"Too Much Drink and No Drive"** The BMA has petitioned the Government to make it an offence to drive with more than 80 per 100 milligrams of alcohol in the blood, approximately 2 measures of spirits or 2 pints of beer. Although this is above the doctors' recommended limit, it is unlikely the Government would legislate on less.

Saturday 20 — **"Training Land"** The army is to buy nearly 100,000 acres of new land to turn into troop training facilities. The *'weariness induced by returning to the same strip at Salisbury Plain, year after year'*, is deemed to have a *'dispiriting effect on troops' enthusiasm.'*

Sunday 21 — **"Death of Malcolm X"** American civil rights activist, Malcolm X, who once called for a 'blacks-only' state in the US was shot dead whilst speaking at a rally in Manhattan. Ten shots were fired, three of which hit Malcolm X in the face.

Monday 22 — **"Yoga Enquiry"** Birmingham is to become the first British local authority to launch an enquiry into yoga and the *'dispersing prana forces'* that it evokes. Questions have arisen over what business the council has to teach people this popular discipline.

Tuesday 23 — **"Spiriting Spirits"** The Distillers Company announced an end to resale price maintenance on its spirits, instead issuing *'recommendations'* over pricing; shortly following the announcement, whisky prices fell in shops by almost 7 shillings.

Wednesday 24 — **"Water Pistol Extinguishers"** Water pistols have been issued to firemen in Newcastle for *'close quarter work.'* They are fired from the hip at a pressure of 400lb per square inch.

Thursday 25 — **"No More Water"** The Lake District Planning Board has decided to oppose Manchester Corporation's proposals to extract a further 45 million gallons of water a day from Windemere and Ullswater lakes.

HERE IN BRITAIN

"Ghost Chair"

A man walked into The Oratory in Brompton, Kensington, and stole *'the ghost chair'*, an artefact brought to Britain from the South American jungle by Colonel Percy Fawcett, an explorer who, shortly after retrieving the strange item, disappeared in the same jungle. No one questioned the man, who was seen leaving the church with the chair on a weekday afternoon. The four-foot piece, made of South American hardwood and padded with crimson leather, was donated to the church by Fawcett's wife following his death.

AROUND THE WORLD

"Too Big for Your Bath"

Rhodesia's Minister of Housing has been criticised for spending £16,000 of taxpayer's money buying and altering a house in Salisbury, Rhodesia, which contains a swimming pool, three car ports and three, £180 chandeliers. Since being bought by Mr Gaunt, the blue Royal Doulton bath has been removed due to the fact that the 205lbs Minister could not lift himself out and, in a move that will not have helped American-Rhodesian relations, Gaunt also removed the chandeliers, describing them as *'the most vulgar things he had ever seen.'*

Co-Educational Schooling

The founders of Bedales, Amy Badley (left) and John Haden Badley (right)

The claim of Mr J.H Badley, at the celebration of his 100th birthday, of founding the first co-educational boarding school has sparked a debate producing a number of counter claims. The Bedales school, founded by Badley in 1893, became co-educational in 1898 after an offer was made by the mother of one of the boys to open *'a house for girls'*, bringing with her a daughter and three others. It was in this haphazard manner that co-education began, with the four girls soon being integrated into the 60-boy-strong year group.

Unlike our European counterparts, whose famous court school of Vittorino da Feltre at Mantua was founded in 1423, there is no landmark date in British history marking the creation of co-ed schooling. The conventions of schools like Harrow, whose rules have remained since 1590, that *'no girls shall be received to be taught in the school'* have remained steadfast, yet others continue to come forward with evidence for their cause. Bunbury Grammar School, established in 1590, has been rejected on the grounds that girls admitted were not to remain *'above the age of nine, nor longer than they may learn to read English.'* Ackworth school, near Pontefract, makes a strong case, as their Quaker morals meant that *'boys and girls alike'* were educated so long as their parents were *'not in affluence'*. Yet, the school has been labelled as 'dual' rather than 'co-educational', due to girls being taught *'to sew, knit and spin'*, parts of the curriculum that excluded boys.

Amongst objections from many other sources, all coming forward to stake their claim as the first, Bedales remains steadfast as the originator, where the foundations were laid of *'an education which should not be shaped by either the shibboleths of the smoking room or by the half-truths of the boudoir.'*

Feb 26th - March 4th 1965

IN THE NEWS

Friday 26 — **"Rebuilding the Leas"** The building, a third of a mile in length with a continuous facade, that fronts the Leas, a grass-covered cliff-top area in Folkstone, has become the centrepiece of development plans for the area.

Saturday 27 — **"Sky Movies Ban"** Following an agreement between 17 members of the International Air Transport Association, *"sky movies"* have been banned to avoid 'wrecking fare-fixing machinery'. The Chairman of B.O.A.C strongly supported the notion, with in-flight entertainment having plagued cross-Atlantic flight fares for many years.

Sunday 28 — **"British TV"** The Treasury has announced that since the beginning of the year, over £1.2 million has been earned through the export of British television and films; the majority of this comes from American Columbia Broadcasting, who air in the US, both the successful series, 'Danger Man' and 'The Saint'.

Mon March 1 — **"Snowploughs to the Rescue"** Snowploughs rescued stranded drivers after blizzards swept across Scotland and the north of England. Trains were cancelled and flights were grounded across the region, and people were forced to stay home from work.

Tuesday 2 — **"Boutique Sheffield"** A £750,000 scheme by private developers to create a *'high-street class of boutique – a little of the best of London'* is to be put forward to Sheffield City Council for approval.

Wednesday 3 — **"Shot Down"** The Conservative motion to retain the death penalty for crimes involving murder by shooting has been defeated at a meeting of the Standing Committee on the Murder (Abolition of the Death Penalty) Bill.

Thursday 4 — **"Cross Now Lights"** A Labour MP has proposed the introduction of a 'Cross Now' light on cars and lorries when slowing at a pedestrian crossing, to signal it is safe to cross.

HERE IN BRITAIN

"A Hairy Situation"

The Post Office has apologised to a fitter after wrongly accusing him of having his wife as a passenger in his official vehicle, a breach of protocol. Upon telling the Office that it was not his wife, they reprimanded him further; to give a girlfriend a lift in the van was worse.

The misunderstanding was resolved following the arrival of the fitter's apprenticed mate, who had long blonde hair. The Post Office would like to clarify that, if efficiency is maintained, the *'length of hair of any member of the union is his own business.'*

AROUND THE WORLD

"5,000 Mile Eavesdrop"

An electronic device capable of transmitting audio data over 5,000 miles was debuted to an astonished Senate committee in Washington. Also on display were new covert *'snooping devices'*; senators were shown microphones concealed within the olive of a Martini, a tie clasp and a packet of cigarettes, and were stunned by lasers that could take television-quality pictures through walls. Many of these devices are advertised in newspapers and available to purchase for regular citizens.

IDEAL HOME EXHIBITION

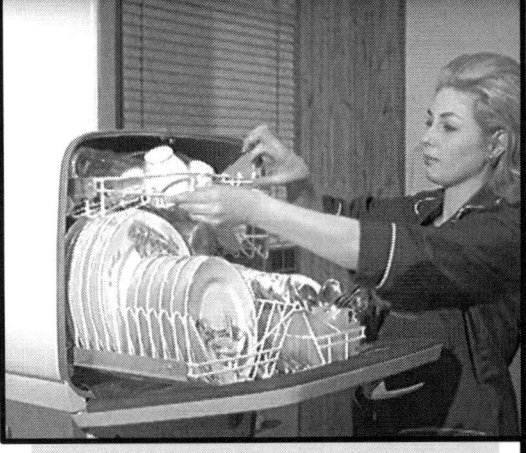

The Ideal Home Show included new household appliances and new home designs

This year's Ideal Home Exhibition, entering its 42nd year, launched stronger than ever, as the sun beat down on the grand hall at London's Olympia. However, the event was overshadowed by a heightened feeling of caution; the exhibition that for so many years has helped save housewives' time, now showcases new machines that are ready to replace her role entirely! The Exhibition has woken up to the fact that the housewife may be faced with an unprecedented wealth of leisure time, much the same as her husbands, and as a result, has taken drastic measures to keep the Exhibition relevant. This year's central exhibit, sponsored by the Daily Mail, is studded with grandeur. Housed in a huge pavilion that would not look out of place next to the Taj Mahal, visitors must pass through an avenue of stalls, brightly lit with synthetic sunlight and blue sky before reaching the nine *'islands of leisure'*, that float on a pool shrouded in darkness and dimly lit. The islands reveal this year's theme: leisure, inside and out. Uncanny life-sized dolls were perched on the islands, each partaking in some form of activity, and the whole thing proved to be baffling to the average visitor.

Nevertheless, the rest of the exhibition did not disappoint. The Edward Drewery steel frame house attracted large crowds with its promise to revolutionise home building. The one on show, clad with grey-brown Yorkshire stone, costs just £7,500 fully furnished, with the option for easily constructed extensions, swimming pools, and even a fully opening roof. The possibility of underfloor heating and a freestanding summer house proved an attractive prospect to potential buyers and developers alike. The houses can be clad in any local material, and several of the two-story buildings can be placed alongside each other to create barracks.

March 5th – 11th 1965

IN THE NEWS

Friday 5 — **"Running Dustmen"** Wirksworth District Council in Derbyshire, following reports that their dustmen run rather than walk, are increasing bonuses by 7s 6d per week. The three-man crew collect 2,000 bins a week, an increase from 1,850 three years ago, despite their hours being cut from 40 to 37.

Saturday 6 — **"Football on Hold"** The weather has forced two FA Cup matches and 11 English and Scottish League games to be cancelled, with 500 roads across the UK still blocked.

Sunday 7 — **"Super New York Flight"** BOAC's Super VC 10 jet made its first cross-Atlantic flight, arriving in New York from London to begin a three-day demonstration. Because of the aircraft's rear-mounted engines, passengers enjoyed a smooth flight despite bad weather.

Monday 8 — **"Berlin Talks"** Prime Minister Harold Wilson enjoyed a drink with members of the Prince of Wales's Own Regiment in Berlin, before engaging in talks with the West German Chancellor about Britain's ongoing commitment to the Rhine Army.

Tuesday 9 — **"Trade Union Army"** An army of 100,000 trade unionists, enough to fill the entire Wembley Stadium, have joined protesting professional footballers following the Football Association's threat to remove the FA Cup final from TV.

Wednesday 10 — **"Goldie Returns"** Goldie, the golden eagle which escaped from London Zoo 12 days ago, has been recaptured after being lured by 8lbs of rabbit flesh.

Thursday 11 — **"Traffic In Babies"** London Authorities have been called out for *'the appalling trafficking of babies'*. Reports say that nursing homes have been established where single mothers can have their babies for a small fee, only for the children to then be sold on for profit.

HERE IN BRITAIN

"Sandbox Discovery"

South African police, accompanied by Chief Inspector Bertram Adams from Southampton, have recovered six of the 20 gold bars missing from the the Capetown Castle liner, now docked in Durban Harbour. The gold went missing in transit between South Africa and Britain last month, and the recovered pieces were discovered in a sandbox just 400ft from the strongroom. The box had been overlooked during the search of the ship after arriving at Southampton, with the £100,000 gold bars stashed *'right at the bottom'*. The thieves cut through a ventilation shaft to gain access to the loot.

AROUND THE WORLD

"Unpatriotic To Travel"

The chairman of the US Senate foreign relations committee has suggested that it would be *'unpatriotic'* for Americans to visit the *'fleshpots'* of Europe on holiday this year. Instead, the senator is encouraging domestic travel, likening New Orleans as an admirable alternative to Paris. He criticised unsolicited European advertisements, involving *'sophisticated debauchery and artistic pickpocketing'* that presents trips to Venice or St. Tropez as irresistible to the American traveller. The State Department is to ensure that getting out of the United States will soon become as hard as getting in.

Sail Training Association

Sir Winston Churchill

The 300-ton topsail schooner sailing boat, being built for training British youth to race in the Tall Ships Race, has been officially given a master, Captain G. NV. T. Griffiths. The 45-year-old Second World War veteran has taught at the King Edward VII Nautical College for the past 12 years and commanded the two training ships associated with the college. There is no more experienced schooner instructor in Britain, nor someone more capable than Captain Griffiths to command the next generation of British sailors. The vessel, to be named the Sir Winston Churchill, with a hull of steel and three aluminium masts, will be the first of her kind built in Britain specifically for youth training. Costing £120,000, she has diesel engines but will rely as much as possible on the power generated by the 7,000 square-footage of sail connected to the masts. She will train 36 young seamen for 14-days at a time; the enterprise is designed to further their sense of self-responsibility, confidence and foster self-reliance.

The schooner has been entered into next year's Tall Ships Race between Falmouth and Copenhagen, an institution running since 1956. The first race, between Torbay and Lisbon, was organised by the Sail Training International Race Committee to showcase the world's remaining Class A Tall Ships, which were thought to be a dying breed in the ever-evolving nautical world. The event was so popular that the committee introduced it as a biennial event, encouraging safe and friendly rivalry between young sailors. When the Duke of Edinburgh became a Patron, the Sail Training Association was born; they have since organised a number of the races, though it is not until next year, with the Sir Winston Churchill, that Britain will officially have her own entry.

March 12th - 18th 1965

IN THE NEWS

Friday 12 — **"Derby Trouble"** Amidst the dispute threatening to remove the FA Cup final from TV, another sporting institution is threatened; Epsom Derby racecourse authority is struggling to reach an agreement with Independent Television to broadcast the event.

Saturday 13 — **"Married Teachers"** The education minister launched a programme encouraging married women to return to teaching. The teacher supply problem can be largely attributed to women teachers marrying and never returning.

Sunday 14 — **"Clacton SOS"** An SOS calling for police reinforcements was too late as hundreds of teenagers swarmed the seaside town of Clacton. Reports of violence and disorder involved new telephones ripped from public call boxes and benches hurled into the sea.

Monday 15 — **"Chance Encounter"** The Queen, visiting her uncle, the Duke of Windsor, in hospital, met the Duchess of Windsor for the first time in 28 years. Mrs Wallace Simpson was the cause of controversy when, in 1936, former King Edward VIII abdicated the throne to marry her.

Tuesday 16 — **"Honesty Box"** A one-day strike of the Underground's 1,500 booking clerks sped up travel across London. Instead of queuing to buy tickets, 'honesty boxes' lay by the turnstiles. It seems, *'thousands of people only travelled within a **6d (2.5p)** distance of Victoria!'*

Wednesday 17 — **"White-Collar Robin Hood"** An offer to return the Goya portrait of the Duke of Wellington, stolen from the National Gallery in 1961, came via anonymous letter. The ransom demands that the painting be displayed at a 5s (25p)-per-view fee, with all proceeds going to charity.

Thursday 18 — **"Plunge 1"** A Soviet Air Force officer has become the first man to leave a spacecraft and float freely in space, spending 20 minutes outside the cabin, secured by a metal 'lifeline'.

HERE IN BRITAIN

"Rob A Blind Man"

The message printed on the cover of the 'Rolling Stones No. 2' record has received such backlash, that the record company has since recalled all copies. *"Cast deep into your pockets for loot to buy this disc of groovies and fancy words. If you don't have bread, see that blind man, knock him on the head, steal his wallet and lo and behold, you have the loot. If you put in the boot, good. Another one sold,"*

The cover made conversation in the House of Lords, who want assurances that the message will be removed.

AROUND THE WORLD

"88-Day Cavewoman"

Josie Laures, who has been living in a cave in the French Alps for the last 88 days, has emerged and been promptly escorted, via helicopter, to the nearest hospital in Nice. Laures, a 26-year-old midwife, was meant to be underground for 90 days, but was pulled out following signs of extreme fatigue.

She was one of many volunteers for experiments to discover the effects of isolation, with findings to be applied to astronauts. She will continue wearing dark glasses for several days, and it will be months before she can resume a normal life.

St Patrick's Day

St. Patrick was possibly a Roman citizen in Britain who was captured and taken to Ireland as a slave in the 4th Century, and later either escaped or was released, before returning as a Catholic priest to convert Irish Druids to Christianity. The 17th of March has been a feast day honouring the saint since 1631, one of many church holidays. Yet, it wasn't until 1903 that the day was officially declared a national holiday in Ireland, and the first St Patrick's Parade wasn't until 1931. Since then, the event has spread across the world, with it now celebrated in more countries than any other national festival. For a long time, St Patrick's Day celebrations were most vigorous in towns outside the homeland, where there was a large contingent of Irish immigrants; the now famous parades began in North America in the 18th Century, not even reaching Ireland until the 1900s. Instead, celebrations in Ireland focus more on lineage than festival, with efforts being made to use the Gaelic language, and lessons in school given about Irish heritage.

Green as an Irish colour dates back to the Great Rebellion of 1641 when patriots revolted against the English crown, using a green flag with a harp as an emblem. Throughout the 19th Century, many Irish would wear a 'St Patrick's Day Cross', made from coloured ribbon with a green rosette in the centre. Today the parade resembles a river of green, winding its way through streets across the world, featuring leprechauns, giants of fable, huge banners and the inevitable tick-a-tape. Traditional food on the day is soda bread and corned beef paired with cabbage, a staple of a stereotypical Irish diet. And of course - no Irish celebration would be complete without the ubiquitous glass of Guinness!

March 19th – 25th 1965

IN THE NEWS

Friday 19 — **"Rembrandt's *Titus*"** Rembrandt's painting of his son *Titus* has been sold at Christie's London Auction House for 760,000 Guineas, a British record. The winning bid was made by the California-based Norton Simon Foundation, who will ship the painting to the US.

Saturday 20 — **"Testing Testers"** A 430,000-strong backlog on young driver tests is to be reduced following the appointment by the Ministry of Transport, of 150 new driving examiners. Two million tests were conducted last year.

Sunday 21 — **"Chicken Run"** 2,500 live chickens were given away by a local farmer in Sussex, in protest against the Government's agricultural price review. The farmer, like many others, *'cannot afford to go on losing money on chickens, each of these costs me 10/- a week'*.

Monday 22 — **"Nuclear Camera Recovery"** After a week of searching, three men made the trip inside a reactor at the West Cumberland atomic energy establishment to retrieve a dropped camera, which fell during refuelling.

Tuesday 23 — **"Order of the Merit"** Dr Dorothy Hodgkin, winner of the 1964 Nobel Prize for Chemistry, has become the second woman to be appointed to the Order of the Merit, which at any time, is limited to 24 members. The first woman was Florence Nightingale in 1907.

Wednesday 24 — **"As Never Seen Before"** The Ranger 9 space probe sent back never-before-seen images of the moon as it descended onto the lunar surface; America watched on, as the images were streamed live to televisions across the US.

Thursday 25 — **"Tons of Business"** An order by Shell International Marine for two £6 million, 90,000-ton tankers, has been won by the Tyneside yard of Swan, Hunter and Wigham Richardson against fierce competition.

HERE IN BRITAIN
"Driving Priorities"

In a survey of the British motoring market, Odham's Press research division found that a heater and a radio are among items that feature higher on priority lists than safety belts. The heater, in first place, is followed by wing-mirrors, important to 69% of people; then fog lamps, 30%; spot lamps, 26%; seat covers, 22%; and radios, receiving 9%. Just one in ten cars on British roads are fitted with seat belts, half of those fitted with radios. The survey also showed that motorists aged over 55 were less concerned about belts than younger generations.

AROUND THE WORLD
"Shoeshine Boys"

To stay in business, Lebanese shoe shiners may be forced to invest in seats for street customers following new Government legislation stipulating that shoes may only be cleaned once taken off, to *'protect the dignity of the bootblack.'*

Beirut's street shoeshine boys barely have the money for a stool for themselves, let alone for their customers, and the new policy will affect them hardest. Many households now have their own personal *'boots'*, who go to their homes to clean the family footwear; this *'preserves the dignity'* of both parties.

The 1,400-ton timebomb

Astonishing sonar image of wreck that could wipe out Kent port at any moment

For twenty years, the 7,146-ton American ammunitions ship the *SS Richard Montgomery* has rested on the seabed of the shallow waters off Sheerness in North Kent, where, at low tide, its masts protrude above the surface. The ship, containing what is estimated to be 1,400 tons of explosives, has been deemed too dangerous to move every year since its grounding on August 20th, 1944. This conclusion remains the same following a report by the Port of London Authority in conjunction with the Home Office that began last Autumn. Although it was affirmed that the ammunition was no-more dangerous than the last review in 1952, indeed an explosion was deemed less likely, it was still recommended that the wreck not be tampered with.

The *SS Richard Montgomery* was built in 1943 in Jacksonville Florida, as part of the mass—production of 2,700 supply ships, designed to give vital aid to the European war effort. When the ship made its maiden voyage to the UK, scheduled to then sail on to Cherbourg, it was laden with over 7,000 tons of ammunition; after arriving in the Thames Estuary, the ship was told to wait for the formation of the convoy at the Great Nore anchorage before making the journey across the Channel. However, the SS Montgomery ran aground on a sandbank 250 metres out from Sheerness. Through a valiant effort by port workers, merchants and the Navy, more than half the cargo was unloaded by the time the ship began sinking, after a crack appeared in the hull; the mission was finally abandoned as the ship became ever more flooded. By day five of the salvage effort, the SS Richard Montgomery was completely submerged, where it has laid ever since.

March 26th – April 1st 1965

IN THE NEWS

Friday 26 — **"TSR 2"** The BAC TSR 2 strike and reconnaissance plane, has made its first unaccompanied flight following month-long checks on the engines. Up until now, the aircraft has only flown with a chase plane.

Saturday 27 — **"Farmers' Protests"** A six-year-old Jersey cow took the salute at a farmer's protest parade in Sussex where 80 farm tractors and other vehicles blocked the A22 London to Eastbourne Road for over a mile and a half. Protests at government price changes were held in many towns.

Sunday 28 — **"Oil Slick Sinks"** Most of the seven-mile long, by three-mile-wide, oil slick caused by two tankers colliding 10 miles off the Sussex Coast has been cleaned. A naval squadron worked for several hours spreading the area with Gamlen, a chemical that sinks oil.

Monday 29 — **"Forest Fire"** Seventy foresters and fifty firemen fought along a two-mile front to combat a forest fire in Snowdonia National Park. The fire caused thousands of pounds worth of damage to the Forestry Commissions' plantations.

Tuesday 30 — **"No Drinks More Drugs"** Although drunkenness amongst young people is falling, according to reports, drug-taking is becoming more serious. A study by the Christian Economic and Social Research Foundation revealed that many drug-users often cannot afford to drink as well.

Wednesday 31 — **"Tin Detector"** New equipment to search for fresh tin reserves in Cornwall will enable the metal to be detected in just two hours, rather than the current 12.

Thurs 1 April — **"Well-Seasoned Traveller"** A Tipton industrialist has become the first person to be issued an honorary season ticket by British Railways' London Region. Over the last 43 years, the gentleman has travelled over 335,000 miles by rail.

HERE IN BRITAIN

"Radio Pirates"

The former SS Frederica, now known as *Radio Caroline,* has been pushing out more exuberant than usual music from five miles off the coast of the Isle of Man, where she is anchored. As the radio station's first birthday came around, upbeat pop music played by the 17 disk jockeys set their mood whilst under threats of blockades and boarding parties. The *"Caroline boys"* however, are popular with the town, where they spend money and attract crowds of teenagers wanting autographs.

AROUND THE WORLD

"No Payments For The Dead"

In Naples, the traditional element in southern religious life, the practice of saying prayers for the dead in return for payment, has been forbidden by the Vatican. The origins of professional prayers, like the professional mourners whose voluble sobs and groans are another feature of southern graveyards, are almost certainly pagan. So far, the order applies only to paying for prayers, but the intention is to try to remove all emotional excesses which accompany the southern cult of the dead.

April Fool

Celebrating April 1st is not a modern custom, as it dates back to the 16th century when Catholic countries in Europe switched from the old Julian calendar, where New Year began with the Spring Equinox around April 1st, to the Gregorian calendar with the New Year celebrated on 1st January. People who continued to celebrate the New Year at the start of April were called 'April fools'.

In the Middle Ages it became accepted to play pranks on people on that day. It is recorded that in 1698, several people were tricked into going to the Tower of London to see the lions being washed! In Britain, a trick is revealed by shouting "April fool!" at the recipient, but only until noon, after which time it is no longer acceptable, in fact, after midday, the trickster becomes the fool! In Scotland the day is called Gowkie Day, for the gowk, or cuckoo, a symbol of the fool.

The custom isn't unique to our country. Some people celebrate it just as a special day, with family and friends and special foods. But for many it is a day for superstition, playing tricks or telling lies. In Iran, it is called '*Dorugh-e Sizdah*' which translates as "getting rid of 13," celebrated on the thirteenth day of the Persian New Year. In France, Belgium and Italy, paper fish are stuck to people's backs, making them 'Poisson d'Avril' or April fish. In Spain some towns have a big food fight, while in Germany they merely resort to shouting April! April! at each other, rather like a verbal 'thumbing your nose'. In Poland, serious activities are usually avoided as every word spoken could be untrue. Back in 1683 a treaty was actually backdated to March 31st to avoid any doubt that it was genuine.

April 2nd – 8th 1965

IN THE NEWS

Friday 2 — **"Affordable Motoring"** New garages across the country are delivering cheaper petrol to thousands of motorists. The sign, a circle with two wavy lines, is trademark of Imperial Chemical Industries, and will advertise petrol that is 7d cheaper than competitors.

Saturday 3 — **"Strike Warning"** 800 striking toolmakers from the Pressed Steel Company have been warned that, if they fail to return to work, 50,000 jobs across the automotive industry will become at risk. Management appealed to the strikers' humanity, in a bid to prevent colleagues from losing their jobs.

Sunday 4 — **"TSR2 Scrapped"** The Cabinet was summoned to discuss the fate of the TSR-2 British *'wonder bomber'*. Harold Wilson met his Ministers at 10 Downing Street before the decision was made to cancel the project.

Monday 5 — **"Applications Flying In"** 500 enquiries a week flood the Royal Australian Air Force, with 1,000 applications coming from Britons. The recruits will be offered free passage to Australia and are only disqualified if over 42 years old, or have a large family.

Tuesday 6 — **"Early Bird Rises"** 'Early Bird', the first commercial communications satellite, was launched into space from Cape Kennedy, Florida, and monitored from Goonhilly Down in Cornwall. The satellite orbits 22,300 miles above the Atlantic.

Wednesday 7 — **"Cigarette Vending Machines"** Following the increase in tobacco duty, the packets of 10 cigarettes supplied in vending machines by the Imperial Tobacco Co., are to stay the same price, but hold just 9 cigarettes.

Thursday 8 — **"BMC Showcase Hall"** The British Motor Corporation's new commercial vehicle exhibition hall, a *'showcase for export'* opened at Longbridge. The 38ft, circular building, made from glass and concrete, can hold 3,300 cars.

HERE IN BRITAIN

"A Golden Legacy"

To the traditional English butler, *'a man who has managed a distinguished household for long enough to merit reward'*, should not stoop to any action so vulgar as applying for severance pay when his employment ceases.

The new Redundancy Payments Bill entitles butlers, chauffeurs and gardeners to a week-and-a-half's pay for every year of service. However, things are expected to continue in their traditional manner, where a *'golden legacy'* is the reward for years of quality service.

AROUND THE WORLD

"Lion's Dispute"

Six performing lions, five chimpanzees, four trained dogs and a Shetland pony remain stranded in Beirut amidst ongoing arguments between creditors and a French circus. Demands by claimants resulted in the animals being confiscated upon arrival in Lebanon.

It was argued that the animals were the property of their keepers, not the circus, and as a result the 70-year-old blind Swiss owner of the chimps, dogs, and pony was flown out to take care of the animals.

PENNY BLACK STAMPS

Commemorative stamps are to be issued honouring the life of wartime Prime Minister Sir Winston Churchill, who died in January, and they will feature a portrait of Sir Winston alongside that of the Queen. The addition of the head of a non-monarch on the postage stamp has only happened once before in British history, when stamps were produced to commemorate playwright William Shakespeare in 1964. Britain is still the only country exempt from having to bear their country's name on their stamps, the head of the monarch enough to confirm its United Kingdom source.

Britain pioneered the first postage stamps in 1840, with the world's first adhesive ones, the *Penny Black* and *Two Pence Blue,* showing the head of Queen Victoria. Letter sending had been a difficult matter before then, and for many years, the privilege of sending messages had been the prerogative of royalty, leading merchants and universities. Even when the letter service became publicly accessible in 1635 under Charles I, it was not cheap and local needs were not addressed. In 1680, English merchant William Dockwra introduced a London penny post, but this was found to be illegal, and closed after two years. The idea was soon reinstated by the Post Office, with many other local penny posts following.

Various changes have been made to the postage stamp since its incarnation in 1840: stamps used to come in sheets and scissors had to be used to transfer a single stamp to the page. This was changed in 1854, when the perforated edge completed trials, allowing stamps to be easily separated from one another with their jagged sides. The colour also proved to be an issue with the original Penny Black and the colour was changed from black to a reddish-brown in 1841.

It was hoped that Sir Winston would be honoured with this privilege for his 90th birthday, but he died before they were finalised and instead, they form a posthumous commemoration of the life of Britain's greatest wartime Prime Minister.

April 9th – 15th 1965

IN THE NEWS

Friday 9 — **"Livingston"** In a bid to restore a *'healthy economic balance in Scotland's central belt'*, details of the proposed 'anvil shaped' town of Livingston have been published. A population in excess of 100,000 should create 45,000 jobs.

Saturday 10 — **"Petrol Pump War"** One by one, oil companies announced petrol price cuts, threatening all-out war at the pumps. Shell, BP and National led the way, with Agip, Murco and Curfew quickly following suit.

Sunday 11 — **"Rocket Mouse"** *Cyclone,* a 4ft 8in rocket, arrived in London as part of a London Science Club experiment. The instrument, designed to carry a mouse to 5,000ft, was a gift from a science club in Bordeaux.

Monday 12 — **"Doping Dogs"** After a month-long investigation, it was found that at least 92 of the 120 dogs at a kennel in Rochester were being doped. The investigation was triggered after a number of dogs fell ill at the same time.

Tuesday 13 — **"The Eleventh Hour"** Two last minute pay settlements reached between British European Airways and the Pilots Union meant that all services would run on time over Easter. Notices for the planned 24-hour strike were revoked the day before the holidays began.

Wednesday 14 — **"Second Dartford Tunnel"** After a review of the Dartmouth Tunnel's first 16 months in operation, Kent and Essex Councils have advised the building of another, before the first reaches its maximum daily capacity of 39,000 vehicles.

Thursday 15 — **"The Show Won't Go On"** A clash with the Kirkaldy Links Market, the largest street fair in Britain, the Carnegie Festival Orchestra sold just 11 tickets for their evening symphony performance, causing it to be cancelled. The venue could seat 1,000.

HERE IN BRITAIN

"Pills for Pigeons"

With the growing *'pigeon menace'* in Grimsby, the chairman of the housing committee has suggested the use of contraceptive birth pills to kerb the growing population. *'No one could possibly object to that, not even the pigeons'*, he said, as he proposed the solution to the estates committee, *'they can still mate, but they will not be able to produce more pigeons.'* He put the idea forward after all other methods they had tried, had failed, saying *'I think these pills would be ideal'.* Experiments in Berlin are already ongoing over the viability of the suggestion.

AROUND THE WORLD

"Elephant Trunk Twisters"

'Twisters hanging out of the clouds like elephant trunks' killed at least 223 people and caused millions of dollars worth of damage when nearly 40 tornadoes struck mid-western US states and was the worst natural disaster in Indiana's history.

The tornado first struck when thunderstorms broke after a pleasant, warm Sunday afternoon. By late evening they had swept through all six states of the Great Lakes and Ohio valleys, before moving east and south-east in a burst of spectacular storms as far as the Atlantic coast.

Wellcome Medical Museum

certain CURE for the BITE of a MAD DOG.

LET the Patient be blooded at the Arm nine or ten Ounces.

Take of the Herb call'd in Latin *Lichen Cinereus Terrestris*, in English *Ash-colour'd Ground Liverwort*, clean'd, dry'd, and powder'd, half an Ounce.

Of black Pepper powder'd, two Drachms.

Mix these well together and divide the Powder into four Doses, one of which must be taken every Morning, fasting, for four Mornings successively, in half a Pint of Cow's Milk warm. After these four Doses are taken, the Patient must go into the Cold Bath, or a cold Spring or River, every Morning fasting, for a Month: He must be dipt all over, but not stay in (with his Head above Water) longer than half a Minute, if the Water be very cold. After this he must go in three Times a Week for a Fortnight longer.

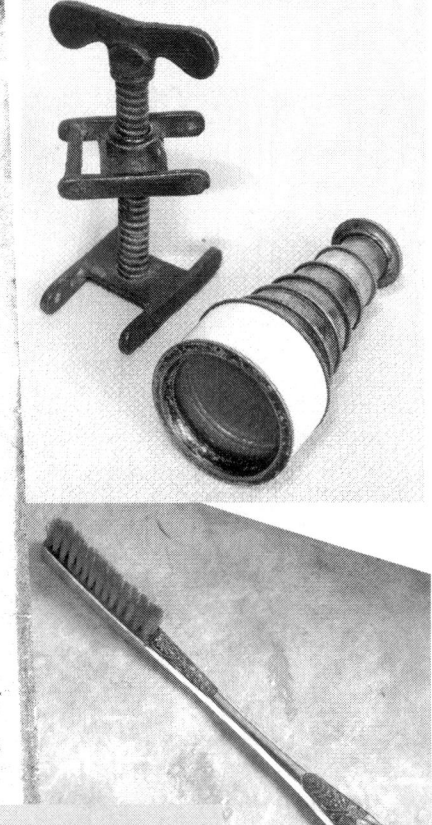

Nelson's Spy Glass and Tourniquet (top). Bonaparte's Toothbrush (Bottom)

An unused, ornate silver gilt toothbrush owned by the Emperor Napoleon, and a blind man's watch used by the Duke of Wellington to help him tell the time in the dark were just some of the obscure items on display at a new gallery in the Wellcome Historical Medical Museum. Although not pivotal devices in altering the course of history, a toothbrush embossed with the imperial signature of one of history's most ferocious leaders drew large crowds on the exhibition's opening day. It intrigued many to learn that Napoleon liked his toothbrush with medium-soft bristles, yet due to their upright nature, it is unclear whether he ever actually used it.

The tourniquet used to amputate Admiral Nelson's arm was accompanied by detailed writings of Sir William Beatty, the surgeon on board Nelson's ship, HMS Victory. He describes how the Admiral was *'mortally wounded in the left-breast by a Musquet ball supposed to be fired from the Mizen top of La Redoubtable'*. All of the items on display were donated to commemorate the 150th anniversary of the Napoleonic wars, but many were focused on early medical breakthroughs of the time. Cures for the *'bite of a mad dog'* included packets of strange powder of which *'as much as will lay on a sixpence'* was to be mixed with *'a large spoonful of the sharpest vinegar made hot.'* Other, more scientific studies were on display, including a first edition of Edward Jenner's theory of vaccination, and the original stethoscope of René Laennec, its inventor.

A fusion of the medicinal and the political, the exhibition also displayed a number of satirical cartoons from England when the Napoleonic threat was at its peak. Many poked fun at politicians, presenting them as bumbling doctors unable to fix the nation nor ward off the *'disease'* that was Napoleon.

APRIL 16TH - 22ND 1965

IN THE NEWS

Friday 16 — **"Ever Ready Army"** For the first time since the inception of the army's Ever Ready Reserve Scheme three years ago, 175 members were called up for service in the Middle East, the Far East and Cyprus.

Saturday 17 — **"No More Circulars"** The ending of the *'household delivery service for unaddressed mail'* came as a victory for the Post Office Workers Union, after its unpopular introduction by the Conservatives to raise revenue for the service that was losing money.

Sunday 18 — **"Gateway to the Lakes"** The Lake District received their first taste of what 110 miles of motorway through the Midlands means for the area's Easter tourism. Nose-to-tail queues spanning 12 miles along the M6 met narrow gridlocked Lake District roads.

Monday 19 — **"Mods and Rockers"** This Bank Holiday Monday, 500 scooter-riding-youths rode through Brighton centre, where 43 were arrested for carrying offensive weapons or for disorderly behaviour. Police had struggled to keep the teens penned on the shingle beach.

Tuesday 20 — **"Rescue Pirate Radio"** An American pilot who bailed out over the North Sea landed just 100ft from the pirate radio ship Galaxy. He was picked up and taken to Harwich, where he was quoted saying *'pirate or no pirate – I've never been so glad to see a ship'*.

Wednesday 21 — **"Unemployment Pay by Post"** Selected exchanges across the country will pay unemployment benefits and national insurance grants by post, as an experiment to improve the status of those seeking work.

Thursday 22 — **"Ernie's Mate"** The premium bond business boomed to such an extent that Ernie, the Electronic Random Number Indicator Equipment, was equipped with a 'mate', Leo 326. Although capable of dispensing 48,000 prize numbers each month, Leo will store the 128 million documents containing bondholders' information.

HERE IN BRITAIN

"Keeping A Promise"

Although the railway station at Apperley Bridge near Bradford has become the latest to close under the Beeching Plan, British Railways will keep a pledge made to a local school 120 years ago. The boys will retain their 'train spotting' rights with a specially constructed hole in the wall. Although trains will no longer stop at the station, the students at Woodhouse Grove School will still be able to watch them speed past, feeding the school's 'thriving rail enthusiasts society.' The station's land was sold to the railway in 1845 by the school's governors.

AROUND THE WORLD

"Selective Migration"

The United States is to amend a long-established discriminatory immigration policy against English starlings and sparrows, birds which had hitherto been put on the prohibited list. The Department of the Interior will remove restrictions on not only English birds, but also flying foxes, mongooses and European rabbits, instead placing prohibitions on previously unregulated animals like injurious fish, molluscs, and Indian wild dogs, all of which now require a permit; surprisingly, man-eating piranha fish will still be allowed free access.

BIDDENDEN MAIDS

On Easter Monday morning, the village of Biddenden in Kent is the scene of a curious old custom called the Biddenden Maids' Charity. In normal times, tea, cheese and loaves of bread are given to the local widows and pensioners from the window of the Old Workhouse. Large amounts of Biddenden Cakes, baked of flour and water, so hard as to be inedible to allow better preservation as souvenirs, are distributed among the crowd of tourists and spectators, each cake bearing the effigy of the Biddenden Maids, two women whose bodies appear to be joined together.

According to tradition, Mary and Eliza Chulkhurst, were born to fairly wealthy parents in 1100 and their bodies were joined at the hips and shoulders. Although, by necessity, close friends, one source states that they sometimes disagreed in minor matters, and had 'frequent quarrels, which sometimes terminated in blows.' In 1134, after 34 years, Mary was suddenly taken ill and died and it was suggested that Eliza should be separated from her sister's corpse by a surgical operation, but she refused with the words, *"As we came together, we will also go together"*, and herself died six hours later. It is from this point that Biddenden's charitable tradition supposedly started - with the sisters pledging the profits from the 20 acres of land they owned be used to provide a dole of bread, cheese and beer to the poor each Easter.

Doubts have been cast on the truth of the old legend, but there is still a demand for the cakes and the bread – made to the archaic quartern loaf size - although in this wartime year of rationing, the cheese has been substituted with cocoa. True or not, the wrought iron village sign shows the Biddenden Maids.

April 23rd – 29th 1965

IN THE NEWS

Friday 23 — **"More May Follow"** 1,700 people have been made redundant so far by the British Aircraft Corporation following the government's decision to cancel the TSR 2 rocket project. In accordance with the new Severance Pay Bill, workers will receive at least half-a-weeks' pay for each week of company service.

Saturday 24 — **"Pennine Way"** The Pennine Way official opening ceremony took place in the Yorkshire Dales, attended by hundreds of walkers. The 150-mile route incurs more accumulative elevation than scaling Mount Everest.

Sunday 25 — **"Boot's Library"** Chemist chain Boots are to close their library service, first established in 1899. During their peak in the Second World War, the library had over one million subscribers, but numbers now barely reach 140,000.

Monday 26 — **"Dive out of Destruction"** The pilot of a Viscount airliner with 42 people on board made a series of dives over the Channel to free its jammed undercarriage. After two and a half hours, the wheels locked into position and the plane landed safely at Bournemouth.

Tuesday 27 — **"Secret Measures"** Police are implementing secret methods to curb railway hooliganism, amidst an increase of lines being blocked with concrete slabs, heavy pieces of wood, bicycle parts and even milk crates.

Wednesday 28 — **"Stand-Up Row Over Sit-Down Tea"** An unsanctioned tea break at a British Motor Corporation tractor plant in Scotland meant that workers were meant to stay standing up; when one man decided to sit, refusing to get up before he finished, he was suspended, prompting the strike of 500 factory workers.

Thursday 29 — **"Gasworks Blast"** An explosion at a Swansea gasworks depot shattered windows across the district and threw pedestrians, on the streets nearby, from their feet; hundreds were evacuated in the fear of a second explosion.

HERE IN BRITAIN

"The Homely Look"

Gone are the days of army barracks resembling a prison block rather than paid-for accommodation. The opening ceremony of the army's latest new-style camp in Maidstone, Kent, revealed living conditions more akin to a modern motel.

The brightly coloured buildings lay nestled within pockets of trees, where the four-to-a-room dormitories are equipped with personal bedside lights, tables, armchairs and basins. The soldiers clean their rooms themselves and they appear as 'orderly' as under the old regime.

AROUND THE WORLD

"Andaman Sea Valley"

Scientists in Washington D.C. have discovered an undersea valley stretching 600 miles in length and reaching 25 miles wide, between the towering mountain peaks of the Andaman Sea in the Indian Ocean.

Beginning just three miles below the surface at the northern tip of Sumatra in Indonesian, the valley finishes 250 miles southwest of Burma. The valley was formed by the *'fracturing of mountain ranges'* during a prehistoric volcanic eruption, and is still within an active volcano zone.

ORDER OF THE GARTER

Lord Brookeborough, former Prime Minister of Northern Ireland, and Lord Bridges, Secretary to the Cabinet from 1938 to 1946 have become the latest of esteemed gentlemen to be appointed Order of the Garter, filling two vacancies opened up by the death of Sir Winston Churchill and Lord Alexander of Hillsborough. The pair fill two of the four remaining spaces to the exclusive order, to which appointments are typically made in recognition of national contribution or service to the Crown. Membership is capped at 24, excluding members of royal families.

The Order was founded in 1348 by King Edward III, who was fascinated with the legends of King Arthur. After defeating the French at the Battle of Crecy he founded a College of St George at Windsor – a community of priests and 24 knights, each provided with a stall in the chapel. Women were originally associated with the Order in the Middle Ages, but this was discontinued until 1901, when Queen Alexandra became the first Lady of the Order for over 400 years. The Sovereign can exclude members who have taken up arms against the Crown; in 1942, because of their hostilities during World War II, Emperor Hirohito of Japan was struck off the list of Garter knights and the Japanese imperial banner was removed from St George's Chapel.

Appointments are announced on 23rd April, which is St George's Day, and Garter Day takes place in June. After the Investiture ceremony, lunch is served in the Waterloo Chamber and then the procession makes its way to St George's Chapel for a service, accompanied by the Heralds and the Yeomen of the Guard all wearing full ceremonial robes and uniform. The public crowd into the streets of Windsor to see this historic spectacle, one of the major events in the 'royal watcher's' calendar each year.

April 30th – May 6th 1965

IN THE NEWS

Friday 30 — **"Michelangelo World Tour"** One of the Royal Academy's greatest treasures, Michelangelo's *Virgin and Child* sculpture is to embark on a world tour, the insurance for which will cost £3 million. The artwork has been offered to Moscow, Amsterdam, Rome, Paris and Washington for display.

Sat May 1 — **"Coughing Cavalry"** The Queen's guard in Whitehall is, until further notice, to be on foot rather than horseback due to the majority of the Household Cavalry's 200 horses having a coughing epidemic.

Sunday 2 — **"First Time"** For the first time ever, Liverpool won the F.A. Cup, beating Leeds United 2-1 at Wembley Stadium. As the club paraded the trophy through the city streets to a crowd of 250,000 people, 134 bus drivers staged a lightning strike, stranding many supporters.

Monday 3 — **"Televised Tracing"** Three hundred million television viewers in Europe and America were urged to help Scotland Yard find the four cockney Englishmen suspected in the Great Train Robbery. The appeal was issued by the world's first commercial satellite, Early Bird.

Tuesday 4 — **"Her Honour"** Judge Elizabeth Lane made legal history as the first female deputy chairwoman in the history of the Inner London Sessions.

Wednesday 5 — **"Double-Decker Piccadilly Circus"** A two-level Piccadilly Circus, with a pedestrian concourse over ground-level traffic, has been suggested by the commission appointed by the Ministry of Transport designed to provide a focal tourist spot in London's West End.

Thursday 6 — **"Computer Sickness"** According to reports, several valuable and senior figures based at Unilever's London headquarters fell ill after the introduction of a computer in their day-to-day roles. The sickness affected programmers and system analysts.

HERE IN BRITAIN

"Wrestling With the Details"

Speaking in Westminster, the Minister for Sport showed a reluctance to set up a control body for the 400 professional wrestlers in Britain. Perhaps all too aware of the fate of referees found caught in the middle of two brawling fighters, the Minister rejected the proposition that a board of control, like that of British Boxing, be established. The objection stems from his refusal to acknowledge professional wrestling's athletic status, calling the events *'rehearsed charades'* that do not fall under his remit. Wrestlers have since decided to set up their own licensed control body.

AROUND THE WORLD

"Kentucky Derby"

Often spoken about as one of America's premier sporting events, the Kentucky Derby of 1965 was staged with its usual excitement and grandeur. The festival is unique in many aspects, often condemned by critics as more a carnival than a race, with two weeks of partying immediately following the *'most exciting two minutes in sport.'* The event continues to be America's most popular horse race, despite being characterised by just two minutes of actual racing. Every year, the carnival draws thousands of spectators, most of whom have no interest in horses or racing.

MAY DAY TRADITIONS

A wheel of cheese in the Randwick Wap ceremony (inset) and Maypole dancing (main).

May Day is a celebration of spring and many of the associated festivities date back to early Medieval times. The 1st of May was traditionally the start of 'Mary's Month' or a month of Christian devotions to the Virgin Mary and was usually declared a holiday allowing everyone to enjoy their inevitable local fair and festivities.

At Oxford's Magdalen Bridge, crowds still gather at first light to hear the May Singing of a hymn, and a madrigal by the choristers of Magdalen College. Later in the day, local Morris dancers entertain those out and about in the city's main streets. In the Gloucestershire village of Randwick, an ancient ceremony known as the Randwick Wap dates back to the 14th century. The Wap is a fair, with a rowdy procession in costume. Three wheels of cheese are elaborately decorated and carried in the procession before being rolled three times round the churchyard. It is an occasion for much quaffing of ale and wine, and although banned in the Victorian period as 'too rowdy and boozy' it was enthusiastically revived two years ago.

Central to most May Day celebrations is the Maypole, which at one time was a large tree in the forest that was decorated in situ, but later was cut down and brought into the village to be decorated with flowers, wreaths, handkerchiefs and ribbons. Complicated dances are performed around it while holding the ribbons attached to the top, which then weave a colourful braid pattern down the length of the pole. During the 16th and 17th centuries, many of the famous village maypoles were destroyed and the celebrations banned as being 'occasions of sin'. However, the late 19th century saw a renewed interest in English customs and May Day became a fixture in the calendar once more.

MAY 7TH - 13TH 1965

IN THE NEWS

Friday 7 — **"Rhodesian Independence"** Rhodesian Prime Minister Ian Smith claimed all 50 seats reserved for 'whites' in the latest elections, giving him the two third majority needed to amend the country's constitution and claim independence from Britain.

Saturday 8 — **"Foiled Escape"** A plot to free James Hussey, one of the thieves involved in the great train robbery, from Walton Jail, Liverpool, was foiled by police and prison staff.

Sunday 9 — **"Yielding Little Fruit"** The installation of a fruit machine in the York Social Club in Windsor Park caused the Queen's chaplain at the park's royal chapel to threaten to resign as he believes it is immoral to entice members to spend their money gambling.

Monday 10 — **"A Warbling Call"** The Postmaster General presented a new and inscribed 'Trimphone' to the purchasers of Britain's ten-millionth phone. According to the Post Office, the Trimphone does not ring, *'it warbles'*.

Tuesday 11 — **"Enterprise Neptune"** The Duke of Edinburgh called the National Trust launch of Enterprise Neptune, a £2 million project designed to preserve 2,000 miles of British coastline, *'a burst of renewed hope'* for the country.

Wednesday 12 — **"Hard Landing"** Russia's Lunik 5 space craft hit the moon harder than intended, raising a sea of cloud from the moon's barren surface. Reports from Russia stated, *'the capsule failed to achieve the planned 'soft landing'*.

Thursday 13 — **"Missing Balloons"** Nine of the ten balloons that took part in the first free balloon race in Britain for 50 years failed to reach the end, forcing the organisers of the event to search for two hours to locate the missing balloons. In some cases, villages in Oxfordshire were left without power after balloons crashed into electricity lines.

HERE IN BRITAIN
"Moving House"

Number 3, High Street, Hereford made its way through the city centre at a speed of one-mile-per-two-days before being parked on the High Town taxi-rank, where it will remain for six months. The 17th Century house was moved to make way for a chain store and will be transported back and integrated into the new structure when complete. It was debated for many days how best to preserve the historic top storeys of the house before the £6,000 project was finally decided upon. The house is mounted to a wooden frame by four steel joints.

AROUND THE WORLD
"Early Bird Gets the Worm"

The Early Bird Satellite proved its worth after helping arrest 39-year-old Canadian George Lemay, suspected in connection with a Montreal bank robbery in 1961. A television programme was transmitted from the satellite containing his photograph and information, with the prompt *'a big spender who may be living in the United States.'*

After seeing the broadcast, a boat keeper in Fort Lauderdale, Florida, led police to a 43 ft yacht in the area, where Lemay was found. Upon arrest, Lemay boasted *'well isn't that something? It took a satellite to catch me.'*

EDITH CAVELL

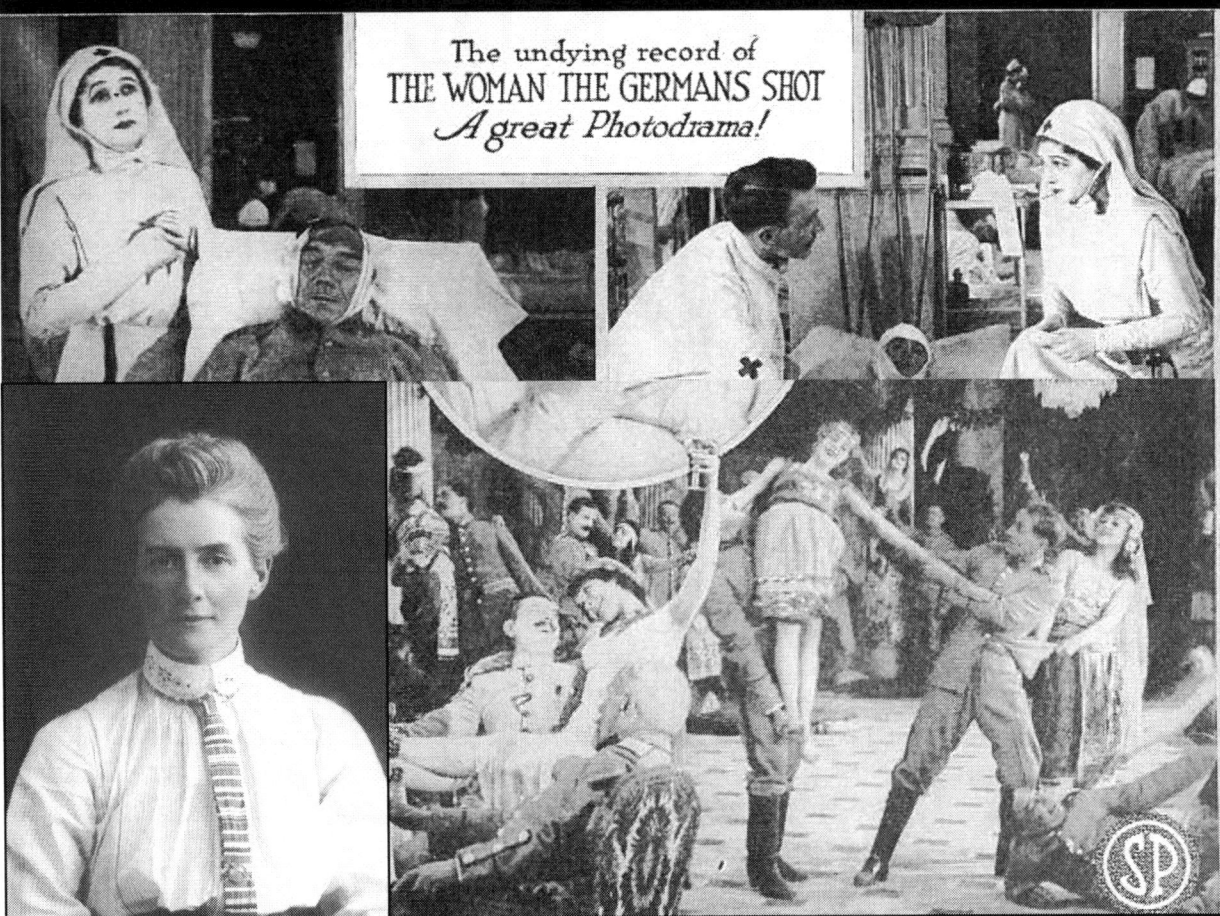

In a lecture to the London Hospital League of Nurses, Cambridge Physicist Professor Clark-Kennedy launched his biography of the life and work of Edith Cavell, who was executed 50 years ago by a German firing squad. On the 50th anniversary of her death, Professor Kennedy's lecture detailed the courageous life led by Cavell, explaining how she helped over 200 allied soldiers flee through Holland in the early part of the First World War, and her legacy as the pioneer of nursing in Belgium.

Cavell began her career as a probationer at The London Hospital in 1896, where she was described as *'somewhat superficial'*, her work *'by no means thorough'*, and her manner *'self-sufficient'*. The first few years of her qualified life were spent in the tough conditions of the St Pancras Infirmary, a hospital well-known for its high fatality rate. After bouncing around rough East London Hospitals, Cavell moved to Belgium, where she became Matron of a new private school for nursing. Cavell developed a reputation for strict discipline and no-nonsense education, as she steadily began to overturn the extremely poor reputation of Belgian nursing. A girl late to class by just two minutes would forfeit her duties for the day, and to be seen having contact with a doctor for any reason other than to discuss a patient was a deadly sin.

During the First World War, Cavell became a beacon of hope for young servicemen fleeing German captivity; her house was always full of allied soldiers, whom she channelled out of the country under the guise of nursing. Eventually, Cavell was caught by the German's, who extracted a complete confession. In court her only defence was that she acted only to maintain life, not to harm the German cause, but nevertheless was executed the next day, reportedly *'glad to die for my country.'*

May 14th – 20th 1965

IN THE NEWS

Friday 14 — **"Last of the Lancasters"** *G For George*, Britain's last airborne Lancaster bomber aircraft, touched town at Biggin Hill airfield in Kent for the final time. The World War Two hero made its final landing following a sentimental 13,000-mile journey from Australia.

Saturday 15 — **"University of the Air"** The BBC has become the first broadcaster to attempt to link educational television with discussion groups and a correspondence course. The project will be used as evidence to support a full-scale 'university of the air'. They are to present a documentary on the range of social work in Britain.

Sunday 16 — **"Danger Roads"** Five hundred miles of British roads where accidents occur *'above average'* are to receive a permanent 50mph speed limit. The Minister of Transport is appealing to the Home Office for support in enforcement.

Monday 17 — **"Colliery Explosion"** 31 men died and a further 13 were injured when an explosion in the Cambrian Colliery, Rhondda, struck miners on a coal face.

Tuesday 18 — **"Robot Ticket Collector"** Acton Town Underground station in London boasts what is believed to be the only robot ticket collector in the world. 'Automatic Bill', named by the staff, *'swallows tickets like oysters, coughing up the bad ones.'*

Wednesday 19 — **"Bonn Crowds for Queen"** On the second day of her German tour, the Queen drove through streets decked with flags and lined with thousands of waving Germans chanting 'Elizabeth!'. Her Majesty then enjoyed lunch with the German Chancellor.

Thursday 20 — **"Robot Eye"** An 'electronic eye' is being developed by scientists at the University of Birmingham so that public services, including fire engines and ambulances, might be able to move around freely during even the thickest fog.

HERE IN BRITAIN

"The Children's Newspaper"

The Children's Newspaper, a British institution since its founding in 1919, published its final edition, ending 46 years of child-friendly and informative news. *'Only the highest standards'* were expected by the paper, who had its own home and foreign affairs correspondents, a parliamentary correspondent, and even a film critic, all authoring stories to keep Britain's children engaged; there were cartoon competitions, and a serial story that dabbled in stamp collecting, railways, and motoring. The paper will be missed by parents and children alike, *'old established but never old fashioned.'*

AROUND THE WORLD

"Medicine Chest"

The *'medicine chest'* clause of a treaty made between Queen Victoria and some Saskatchewan Indian tribes in Canada was cited in court by the defence counsel on their way to a 'not guilty' verdict.

The 1876 treaty was evoked after a treaty Indian failed to pay compulsory premiums for hospital and medical care, a provision made free after the handshake deal between Queen Victoria and the Saskatchewan tribes. *'A medicine chest shall be kept at the house of each Indian agent for the use and benefit of the Indians at the direction of such agent.'*

Runnymede Kennedy Memorial

The British memorial to John F. Kennedy was inaugurated by the Queen, officially granting three acres of British soil to the United States in Runnymede. From the green meadow that houses the memorial it is possible to see Magna Carta Island, the site on which King John signed away his divine sovereignty in 1215, a symbolic nod to Kennedy's liberal politics. Members of the Kennedy family met with the Queen, who led them along a granite path to the memorial. A singular white and rectangular stone, flanked by representatives of both the British and American Navies, records the dates of the late president's life and the famous address from his inaugural speech to the American people about paying any price for the survival and success of liberty.

The Prime Minister spoke on behalf of the trustees of the Kennedy Memorial; Mr Macmillan was in office for only weeks before the President's assassination but did not over exaggerate the profound affect his death had on the Western world; *'one of those rare personalities who seemed born to bridge the gulf dividing races and creeds and help to build the unity of mankind.'*

In a touching speech, Mrs Kennedy made a personal address to the British people; *'I wish to thank the British people for their magnificent gift of a piece of British land in memory of my husband. For free men everywhere. Runnymede is indeed sacred soil. It is the birthplace of our ideals of human freedom and individual dignity in which my husband passionately believed. My husband loved history and what you have done today in his honour would please him more than my words can express. He had the greatest affection for the British people.'*

May 21st - 27th 1965

IN THE NEWS

Friday 21 — **"Non-Toxic Tear Smoke"** The Home Office announced that certain officers of the Metropolitan Police will be equipped with non-toxic tear smoke for use against armed criminals trapped in buildings. The gas will not be used in any other scenario.

Saturday 22 — **"World's Biggest Ship"** Harland and Wolff of Belfast have received an order for what is soon to be the world's largest merchant ship, a 167,000-ton tanker for a Norwegian businessman. The vessel will cost over £5 million and stretch over 1,000 ft long.

Sunday 23 — **"Cutting Living Costs"** The National Union of General and Municipal Workers has become the first trade union to enter the mail order business, hoping to save up to 20% on goods and services for its 800,000 members by dealing with wholesalers and merchants directly.

Monday 24 — **"Homosexual Law Reform"** The House of Lords voted almost two to one in favour of homosexual law reform; under the new legislation, private homosexual acts between consenting adults will be made legal.

Tuesday 25 — **"Welsh Pits Idle"** A strike by pit officials in Wales, whose paramount job is safety, caused more than 65,000 miners to lay idle, paralysing the 85 pits across the region. The strike stemmed from a 'swearing' dispute between workers.

Wednesday 26 — **"Phantom Punch"** The fastest knockout in heavyweight championship history befell Sonny Liston after a brutal right hand by Muhammad Ali *'landed with the thud of a cream puff'*, flooring the former champion just one minute into the first round.

Thursday 27 — **"Prison-Building-Prisoners"** The Government has given the green light for the first prison establishment to be built by prison labour. Eastwood Park detention centre in Gloucestershire will require 100 men and take two years to complete.

HERE IN BRITAIN

"Throwaway Car"

A British design firm is pioneering an extremely compact, five-seater car, from which damaged parts would be thrown away and replaced rather than repaired. Powered by a throwaway engine capable of 50mph, the prototype is just 7ft long (3ft shorter than a Mini), and 5ft wide.

The technical director explained its intended use in under-developed countries, like Pakistan, where *'what we have in mind is something cheap and economical, to replace the scooter and trailer-type rickshaw they are using in these countries'*. Production is to be done in Britain.

AROUND THE WORLD

"Moscow Old Elegance"

Russian designers began a project in Moscow to blend sophisticated western style with the sartorial elegance of the old Russian aristocracy, all within the requirements of mass communist production.

The work of 80 designers was paraded at the House of Fashions in the Soviet capital, where one-of-a-kind prototypes were shown off. The coats drew much attention, the inspiration for which came from the elaborate costumes worn by the noblemen of Peter the Great, lined with fur strips like a knight from the chorus of Boris Godunov.

SCARVES OF HONOUR

One of the eight Scarves of Honour, crocheted by Queen Victoria in the last year of her life, will be presented to the people of Canada by the nephew of one of the original recipients. The scarves were given out at the beginning of the century to soldiers who had distinguished themselves in war to the highest degree; a Victoria Cross was not enough. Instead, nomination for a VC, followed by two further commendations for bravery was a prerequisite for the short list, with final recipients nominated by a vote from fellow soldiers. This scarf will be awarded to the people of Canada for commitment to the Commonwealth and placed in the National War Museum.

Originally, the scarves were made on request by Queen Victoria, who wished to personally reward the bravery of soldiers in the Boer War. Her Majesty crocheted the scarves from khaki coloured Berlin wool, embroidered with the initials 'VRI'. Because of their exclusive nature, the eight scarves were awarded *'to the best all-round men taking part in the South African campaign'*. Four were presented to British units, with the other four going to each Commonwealth country who had supported the South-African war effort.

The scarves remain scattered across the globe, residing in the Queen's Regimental Museum, the National Army Museum in Chelsea, the Australian War Memorial in Canberra, three more as part of private collections and now in the Canadian National War Museum in Ottawa. The nephew of Canada's scarf recipient, Private Richard Thompson, gifted the scarf to the Canadian museum, after his uncle risked his life, under enemy fire to save the lives of others. At the Battle of Paardeberg, he stayed on the battlefield to hold bandages on the throat of a wounded soldier, saving his life in the process.

May 28th – June 3rd 1965

IN THE NEWS

Friday 28   **"Peace in the Coalfields"** It took the Chairman of the National Coal Board just 30 minutes to form a peace formula for the South Wales coalfields after a meeting in Blackpool. 52,000 miners across 85 coalfields have lain idle for four days after a strike by 3,500 under-officials over a swearing incident between a colliery deputy and a young miner.

Saturday 29   **"Visit of the Century"** Thousands of waving Germans greeted The Queen and Duke of Edinburgh aboard the Royal Yacht Britannia as it arrived in Hamburg.

Sunday 30   **"Harbour Dive"** Graham Hill's victory at the Monaco Grand Prix was overshadowed by Paul Hawkin who drove his Lotus out of the chicane and straight into Monaco harbour, the first crash into the harbour during a race since Alberto Ascari 11 years ago.

Monday 31   **"Country Club"** Britain's first country club for trade unionists was unveiled by the Secretary of State for Education and Science. If the idea is successful, then there are plans to roll out further sites across London.

Tuesday 1 June   **"Eight-Level Motorway Link"** The Ministry of Transport disclosed plans for the final motorway link between the M5 and M6; the 64-mile link includes 20 miles of motorway through the built-up areas of Birmingham.

Wednesday 2   **"Stop That Noise!"** A prototype acoustically controlled window was tested in a classroom at a school close to London Airport. When the 'massive noise' of the jets taking off began, the window closed automatically, opening again when the noise abated.

Thursday 3   **"Lorry Spot-Check"** The Ministry of Transport is to drastically increase spot checks on heavy goods vehicles, across the 12 UK traffic areas, 130,000 lorries will be examined in 1965, compared to 117,000 last year.

HERE IN BRITAIN

"Reinterred Duchess"

In a private ceremony at Westminster Abbey, the remains of Anne Mowbray, the child Duchess of York, were reinterred in almost the exact place she was originally laid to rest 500 years ago. Wife of Richard Duke of York, one of the infant princes in the tower, Mowbray was found on a building site in Stepney last December.

Reports say she was moved, in her little lead coffin, from London to a medieval nunnery known as the Abbey of the Minoresses after the Chapel of St Erasmus was demolished in 1502 to build Westminster Abbey.

AROUND THE WORLD

"Cross-Channel Competition"

Competition in the cross-channel ferry market is heating up, with Swedish newcomers, Stena Line, offering not only the first drive-on ferry between the Thames at Tilbury and Calais, but also gambling, bingo, dancing, and 38 varieties of smorgasbord to entertain continental travellers.

Scandinavian entrepreneur, Sten Olsson, is set on making his service the best in the business, with scheduled daily sailings of his 2,800-ton liner 'The Londoner'; the ship can hold over 1,000 passengers and 100 cars and will make the 78-mile round trip each day.

JAM AND JERUSALEM

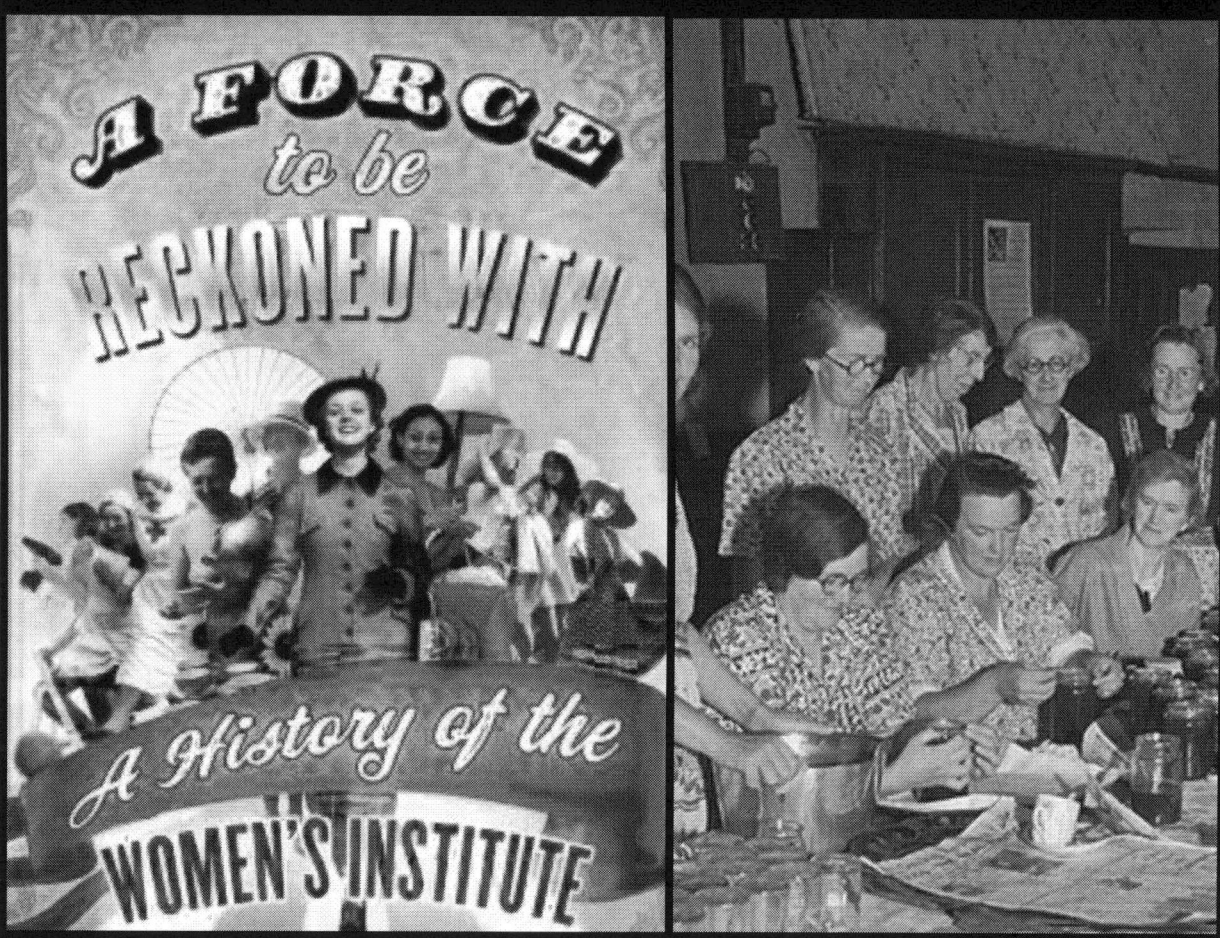

Her Royal Highness the Duchess of Gloucester opened an exhibition entitled *'The Countrywoman Today'*, at the Ceylon Tea Centre, at the beginning of a week of celebrations commemorating the golden jubilee of the Women's Institute. The week's events aimed to best capture the exploits of the group over the last 50 years, the work of women across the country who sought tirelessly to improve conditions of rural life; promoted countless friendships; and provided a remarkably wide range of educational activities for its country members. Both Queen Elizabeth and the Queen Mother attended the first day of the annual general meeting in the Royal Albert Hall, and at the end of the month each one of the 8,717 institutes sent a representative from their ranks to attend a garden party on the lawns of Buckingham Palace.

The Women's Institute was founded In 1897 In Stoney Creek, Canada, by Mrs Adelaide Hoodless, who felt that the death of her infant son was due to her own lack of knowledge of nutrition; after organising a small group set on spreading education and skills for women, the idea soon caught on. The W.I. spread to England around 1915, and by 1918 there were over 800 institutions across the country. That number is now over 500,000 worldwide and since its inception over £180,000 has been raised for the Freedom From Hunger Campaign. During both the First and Second World Wars, the W.I played a vital role in encouraging the growing of food and looking after refugees, and were instrumental in pushing the women's rights agenda at the end of the 1940s. Aside from the Food For Hunger Movement, the W.I. has been involved with all manner of social and domestic programmes throughout the 1950s and 1960s, including the Keep Britain Tidy group and a scheme to replant dying oak trees.

June 4th – 10th 1965

IN THE NEWS

Friday 4 — **"Peace Talks Fail"** Chairman of British European Airways dismissed 300 porters for their *'ludicrous anarchy'*, after a strike paralysed Luton Airport. The chairman said that he would not submit feebly to *'the pressure tactics of a few.'*

Saturday 5 — **"Torbay"** The towns of Torquay, Paignton and Brixham are to be combined under one county of Torbay, announced by the Minister of Housing. The centre will be designed to attract development in the hope of fostering a tourist area of national importance.

Sunday 6 — **"The Church Objects"** Fourteen men, a minister, and several church elders were among a group arrested on the Isle of Skye for blocking the road against the vehicles driving off the first of the Sunday ferries to operate on Skye.

Monday 7 — **"Gemini IV"** The record-breaking American spaceship, Gemini IV, returned to earth after four days in the void during which one of the crew, Major Edward White, floated free in space on an *'umbilical line'* for 20 minutes.

Tuesday 8 — **"Strike Fizzles Out"** The BEA strike lost support when 400 of the eventual 970 who received dismissal notices, returned to work. Normal service was resumed but the daily loss caused by the strike over the Whitsun weekend was £300,000.

Wednesday 9 — **"White Collar Crime"** A number of art galleries in London have been offered works which are thought to be forgeries from an Italian counterfeit ring discovered in Rome last month. Two men have been arrested in Milan in conjunction with the works.

Thursday 10 — **"Automatic Landing"** Passengers on board a BEA flight from Paris to London were told, once they were safely on the ground, that they were the first in the world to have been landed by an *'automatic pilot'*. Passengers reported a *'slightly bumpy landing'*.

HERE IN BRITAIN

"Mixed Manned Ship"

A 4,500-ton, guided missile destroyer, carrying crew from seven different nations, arrived in Portsmouth to test the viability of a multi-lateral nuclear force. The mixed crew aboard the US Navy vessel is made up of British, American, German, Greek, Italian, Dutch, and Turkish seamen, but, in the UK especially, there is little enthusiasm for the project. The mixed man fleet could cost as much as £170 million per year, and British sailors have already complained about their lack of a tot of rum; the compensation for which, is that they are paid US Navy wages.

AROUND THE WORLD

"Wales Window"

A service of dedication was held at a church in Birmingham, Alabama, for the four black Sunday school children who were killed after a bombing by the Klu Klux Klan in 1963. The abhorrent racist action sent shock waves around the world, no more so than in Wales, where the idea for a replacement of the ornate stained-glass window broken during the blast, was dreamt up. The 9ft window, smelted in Wales by John Petts, portrays a black Christ spreadeagled in protest, and the window was unveiled at the ceremony, before a large, predominantly black, congregation.

WHITSUNTIDE

This week, Whit Sunday was celebrated around the world by Catholics, Anglicans and Methodists. This special day is celebrated to commemorate the descent of the Holy Spirit upon Christ's disciples and is the seventh day after Easter or Pentecost, its name deriving from the Anglo-Saxon word 'wit' meaning 'understanding' to celebrate the disciples being filled with the wisdom of the Holy Spirit.

Whit Monday was officially recognised as a bank holiday in 1871 and the day has a special cultural significance in the north-west of England. Many workplaces including factories and cotton mills closed for the whole Whitsuntide week giving workers a holiday and towns held fairs, markets, and parades. Still a major tradition is the 'Whit Walk', when local churches or chapels employ bands to lead traditional processions through the streets. Often the Catholic Sunday schools walk on Whit Friday and the Anglican Sunday schools on Whit Monday bringing in an element of competition in display, dresses and banners! The origin of these processions date back to July 1821 when the children of Manchester commemorated the coronation of George IV and children of all denominations walked in procession from their schools and assembled at Ardwick Green to sing 'God Save the King'.

The Bradford Whit Walk has been held continuously since 1903 and is one of the most popular events on the race-walking calendar, attracting hundreds of entries. At the height of its popularity, it attracted top British race walkers and in the 20s and 30s was recognised as the breeding ground for British Olympians, with winners Tommy Green and Harold Whitlock going on to win Olympic gold medals in 1932 and 1936 respectively. This is also the week for many local brass band contests and workers to take the opportunity to enjoy canal boat rides, go to the races and of course, go to the seaside.

June 11th - 17th 1965

IN THE NEWS

Friday 11 — **"Motor Insurance War"** British Petroleum announced a scheme under which motorists who make three purchases of BP petrol would be given free insurance against the loss of cars through breakdown on a summer holiday.

Saturday 12 — **"Royal Pop Honours"** The Beatles came out on top in the Queen's inaugural *'pop'* honours list which included all forms of *popular entertainment.*

Sunday 13 — **"Public Hovercraft"** The British Railways Board announced to the government, their plans to build the world's first car carrying passenger hovercraft. The £1.2 million project will be launched on the Solent.

Monday 14 — **"Coventry Cathedral"** The discovery of the remains of Coventry's first cathedral, founded over 900 years ago by Earl Leofric and Lady Godiva, was disclosed to the public. They are on the site of a planned refractory building for the current cathedral and time is of the essence to discover what treasures might lie within the remains.

Tuesday 15 — **"Deep-Sea Marine Workshop"** Royal Navy divers descended 600ft for one hour, 18 times, in a series of experiments for deep sea diving ship reclaim. They established a marine workshop on the seabed of the Mediterranean just off Toulon.

Wednesday 16 — **"Cunning Thieves"** A group of thieves put up road signs to divert traffic out of the Strand underpass so that they could ambush a GPO mail van. Eighty bags of registered mail were stolen in the brazen heist.

Thursday 17 — **"Peace Mission"** Harold Wilson will lead a mission of four Commonwealth Prime Ministers to Hanoi, Saigon, Moscow, Washington and Peking to discuss peace in Vietnam. Mr Wilson asserted *'the essential role of the Commonwealth on the world stage.'*

HERE IN BRITAIN

"Tower Weapon Surplus"

The Tower of London is to release more than 1,000 carbines, muskets, rifles, pistols, swords, and bayonets because the basement space where they've been stored for decades is now needed.

The equipment will be sold at auction at Sotheby's. Collectors are most interested in 300 detached sword blades, a nineteenth century airgun, and a Brown Bess musket inscribed with *'Fool Proof Warranted'* are amongst the more valuable items, although buyers have been warned that the three light infantry guns from the 1750s are *'very defective'.*

AROUND THE WORLD

"Islands Come and Go"

Within the space of a week, an island was formed and subsequently destroyed by volcanic eruptions off the coast of Iceland amidst ongoing volcanic storms. Tourists have been using their Whitsun holidays to fly over the new volcano, which has been sending pillars of smoke as high as 3000ft.

Just east of Surtsey, an active volcanic island since 1963, the new volcano's frequent undersea eruptions have seen the creation of a small island that emerged out of 60 fathoms of water. The rapidly solidifying streams of lava, when hardened, form the rocky islands.

The Queen's Coronation BIRTHDAY PARADE
★ TROOPING THE COLOUR CEREMONY ★

Wearing the uniform of the Welsh Guards, who celebrated their 50th anniversary this year, the Queen took the battalion's salute at the annual Trooping of the Colour Parade. After the pomp and ceremony concluded, the Queen was handed her 15-month-old son, Prince Edward, and waved from the balcony of Buckingham Palace. This year's event also marked the last time that Her Majesty rode her beloved horse *Imperial,* before he was retired from active duty. He was also ridden in 1962, and 1964, with a horse named *Doctor* filling in for *Imperial's* absence in 1963.

Trooping the Colour is a military parade that involves the seven army regiments that serve the queen grouped under the umbrella of 'The Household Division' and the ceremony is said to be based on an ancient Roman military practice in which the regimental standard was marched in front of soldiers who would then be able to identify it on the battlefield. Regimental flags of the British Army were historically described as 'Colours' because they displayed the uniform colours and insignia worn by the soldiers of different units.

A regiment's colours embody its spirit and service to the home it represents, as well as its fallen soldiers and before and after each battle, the colour party would 'troop' or march their colours through the ranks so that every soldier could see that the colours were intact. On the battlefield, the flags were used as rallying points and the loss of a colour, or the capture of an enemy colour, were respectively considered the greatest shame, or the greatest glory on a battlefield. For more than 250 years, Trooping the Colour has commemorated the birthday of the sovereign as well as showcasing a display of army drills, music and horsemanship.

June 18th - 24th 1965

IN THE NEWS

Friday 18 — **"Furore Over Beatles Honour"** The Prime Minister has received letters from people who felt compelled to comment on the award of MBE to the pop group, The Beatles. Downing Street said, *'for every one in favour of the award, there were two against.'*

Saturday 19 — **"Drink Drive Law"** The AA were amongst the harshest critics of the Government's proposed new law making it an offence to drive with more than a certain level of alcohol in the blood. The AA Chairman questioned the fairness of the law, given that alcohol affects everyone differently.

Sunday 20 — **"Woodland Census"** A census into the extent of Britain's woodlands is to begin this year, sampling one acre in every seven of the woodlands involved. Forestry commission woods will not be included, as their potential production value information is available.

Monday 21 — **"UN Financial Aid"** Britain has promised a *'voluntary, unconditional, financial pledge'* of $10 million (roughly £3.5 million), to *'help restore the United Nations to Solvency'* and pursue discussions on further peacekeeping arrangements.

Tuesday 22 — **"700th Anniversary of Parliament"** The Queen and Duke of Edinburgh were among 1,700 people gathered in Westminster Hall to celebrate the 700th anniversary of Parliament.

Wednesday 23 — **"BBC Sensitivity"** The Head of BBC Television Drama sent a reminder to producers to ensure they are being sensitive in the treatment of sex, religion and minorities, after reports of 'slipping standards.'

Thursday 24 — **"Railway Vandals"** Elm Park Stadium in Essex became the first railway station to install closed circuit televisions to monitor and catch vandalism. The area is one of the worst affected, where a train was derailed last month whilst travelling at 70mph.

HERE IN BRITAIN

"50 Days at Sea"

The investment into the new generation of big freezer trawlers, whilst paying dividends in terms of catch volumes, is putting a large strain on the industry, as companies are finding it harder and harder to find men willing to go away for months on a trawler.

Nevertheless, Grimsby's newest ship, the Victory, brought in the largest catch ever by a British trawler; 540 tons of mostly Newfoundland cod, worth more than £35,000, which took 50 days to catch. To entice men for these longer trips, companies are offering higher wages and providing more in-comfort.

AROUND THE WORLD

"Cave Women"

Seven women, who have never met, will undertake two-weeks locked together in an underground cave in France. The experiment, organised by a group of Paris doctors, is to test the psychological and physiological effects of prolonged isolation on women.

Their only contact with the outside world will be through two-way telephone with the doctors, who will provide constant check-ups to ensure the women's' safety. They will be provided with camp beds to sleep, sufficient rations for three meals per day, and a torch with meters to record the length of time they had light.

Summer Solstice

There is ongoing maintenance of the stones around Stonehenge and only Druids will be allowed into the enclosure at the ancient site at the summer solstice this year. Usually, Druids, along with a select few members of the public who get there early enough, are allowed through to the enclosure, but this year the government have deemed there to be too much of a risk to allow the general public.

The solstice is a biannual event that occurs once in the summer and once in the winter when the sun reaches its highest point in the sky from either the North or South Pole. The event is especially important in the calendars of the Druids, whose origins date back to early Celtic culture. Druids were often high-ranking priests and healers who held a special place in the Celtic society and in Irish folklore, druids are often described as serving kings and lords as counsellors and are often blessed with magical powers such as being able to see the future or control the weather. The modern Druid movement is more diverse, concentrating on appreciating and 'syncing' with the natural world but the movement was born out of a respect for the ancient beliefs.

Stonehenge, a prime spot for hippy congregation, is a magnet for the Druid movement during the solstice, maybe because of its unique alignment with the movements of the sun and moon which would have given the ancient Druids a special vantage point from which to observe and chart the movements of the celestial bodies, helping them to better understand the natural rhythms of the world around them and a place of healing and rejuvenation. Today's Druids still hold Stonehenge in high regard, a site with a special place in their hearts and minds.

June 25th – July 1st 1965

IN THE NEWS

Friday 25 — **"New Berlin Crisis"** Armed Communist helicopters are being flown over Berlin by the East Germans, and this, the Allies say, endangers the general allied position on which the free access to, and livelihood of, west Berlin depends.

Saturday 26 — **"Slippery Secrets"** The Royal Navy are keeping the secrets uncovered by HMS Reclaim, a deep-sea diving ship, close to their chest and away from British industry, after the ship returned from a six-week Mediterranean excursion. Oil companies are reportedly willing to offer small fortunes for the information.

Sunday 27 — **"Leaking Information"** Religious studies exam questions set by the Oxford Exam Board, have been scrapped after a leak meant that many students got to see them in advance.

Monday 28 — **"Whaling Commission"** The conversation was bleak at the seventeenth annual meeting of the International Whaling Convention, as the Minister of State for Scotland outlined the *'inadequate'* methods of whale conservation.

Tuesday 29 — **"What a Surprise"** Organisers of an appeal for money to buy Britain's first betatron cancer-treatment machine said that they are to buy the identical machine found in a factory at Stafford. Over £135,000 has been raised for it to be placed in Britain's most advanced radiotherapy unit at St. Luke's Hospital, Guildford.

Wednesday 30 — **"Costs of Occupation"** The German Finance Minister has pledged £42 million to support the continued British military presence on the Rhine. This follows rumours of British withdrawal due to struggles with domestic balances of payments.

Thurs 1 July — **"Little Black Boxes"** From today, all new aircraft operated by British airlines must be fitted with *'little black boxes'* that provide permanent records of equipment failures.

HERE IN BRITAIN

"Democracy Plea"

Mrs Perry Edwards, a prospective parliamentary Liberal candidate for Derby South, submitted a scathing letter to British Railways detailing that if the footbridge at the town's railway station wasn't deemed safe enough for Princess Margaret, then it should be repaired for the benefit of all other women too. *'After all, that is democratic'*, said Mrs Edwards, after British Rail washed down the station's steps, and rolled out 20ft of carpet especially for the royal visit, so that the Princess would not *'catch a stiletto heel in the cracks of the footbridge.'*

AROUND THE WORLD

'The Closer He Gets'

The first shampoo-in permanent hair-colouring product for home use by Clairol was called Nice 'n Easy. The advertising tagline, *"The closer he gets...the better you look,"* follows the previous tagline, *"Does she...or doesn't she?"*

Lead copywriter Shirley Polykoff described the Clairol woman as *"Cashmere-sweater-over-the-shoulder type, who's a little prettier than your wife and lives in a house slightly nicer than yours."* In the 1950s, just 7% of American women used hair colour, the popular belief being that it was only actresses, models and women considered promiscuous, who did so.

The Salvation Army

OUR WHITECHAPEL SHELTER.

Over 6,000 members of the Salvation Army attended centenary celebrations at the Royal Albert Hall, with the Queen, the Archbishop of Canterbury, and the Home Secretary. Over the past century, the charity has grown from a small London group to an international institution, and praise was given to the founder, William Booth, in the form of touching tributes by all who spoke. *'He was one of the most remarkable men ... who ever lived',* commented the archbishop, and memoirs flooded in of the work Booth did with schools, the homeless and the poor.

Booth, born in Nottingham, underwent his spiritual awakening at 15 years old, after which he moved to London and started working as a pawn broker in Walworth, but he described this phase of his life as 'lonely'. By 1855 he had married, given up pawnbroking and been ordained as a Methodist priest. His desire to preach took him from church to church spreading the word of revival and abolition of sin. When the Methodist Church requested that he take up an ordinary pastorate, he split with them and continued his travels across East London on his own accord. He founded 'The Christian Mission' programme, the precursor to the Salvation Army, and from there his evangelical mission grew in support and gained the name of 'army'. The movement attracted opposition from orthodox and conformist Christians, who did not like Booth's 'flashy and ornate' message, especially the use of brass bands, but nevertheless by 1888 the ideas had spread throughout Europe and America. A permanent headquarters was established on Queen Victoria Street in London in 1881, which remained for over 60 years until it was destroyed in a German bomb raid. Over £500,000 was raised for its replacement.

July 2ⁿᵈ - July 8ᵗʰ 1965

IN THE NEWS

Friday 2 — **"Costly Coal"** The Government is to write off over £400 million of the National Coal Board's £1,000 million debts, with aims to close uneconomically viable pits at an increasing rate. Over the past eight years the industry has contracted by 30 million tons.

Saturday 3 — **"Magic Eye"** Four Scottish coal pits are to be the recipients of new *'magic eye'* systems, capable of remote indication and control. The new devices which can find faults and put them right, will cost £100,000 to install.

Sunday 4 — **"Congested, Uncomfortable and Inconvenient"** The Ministry of Aviation agreed that these words describe London Airport but say *'they have a major improvements programme in hand and are running an extremely busy airport at the same time.'*

Monday 5 — **"Tea Cut"** More than 100 workers in a Buckinghamshire brush making firm decided to cut out their daily afternoon tea break to instead be able to *'clock off'* at Friday lunchtime.

Tuesday 6 — **"Freak Accident"** 41 British servicemen were killed after an RAF Hastings transport aircraft crashed just minutes after take-off in a barley field just outside Oxford. The aircraft was meant to drop trainee parachutists somewhere over Weston-on-the-Green.

Wednesday 7 — **"School Haircuts"** A 53-year-old bus conductor was fined the maximum by Ascot Magistrates Court for failing to send his son Keith to school for 40 days; the father pleaded not guilty on the grounds that he was told by Keith's headmaster that his son's hair was too long to take part in many activities.

Thursday 8 — **"The Great Escape"** Ronald Arthur Biggs, in Wandsworth Prison for his involvement in the great train robbery, escaped with three other inmates by scaling a 20ft wall. Every police car in London was alerted in what was the largest manhunt of the year.

HERE IN BRITAIN

"Cross Channel Merrymakers"

1,592 jovial men and women boarded the Royal Daffodil pleasure cruiser at Southend-On-Sea bound for Calais. For just £2 7s, they got to spend three hours on the continent on a trip involving *'non-stop festivity'*.

Punters boarded carrying beer by the crate, and the captain's obligatory *'abandon ship'* procedure was drowned out by impromptu pop sessions. Whilst it would be easy to assume that a boatload of British tourists would be a burden to Calais townsfolk, the reality was quite the contrary; shops received booming trade, with few shopkeepers wanting the festivities to end.

AROUND THE WORLD

"Blame it on the Drink"

According to Russian reports, 65% of murders, 71% of assaults producing grievous bodily harm, and 90% of all vandalism are carried out by persons under the influence of alcohol. A push for *'resolute action against drunkenness'* has been published by Russian government newspaper, Izvestia.

The proposed measures include: making drunks responsible for the cost of medical assistance in intoxication related incidents; police ability to impose fines for drunkenness; and to encourage trade unions to penalise excessive drinking.

WIMBLEDON CHAMPIONSHIP

Australian, Margaret Smith won the 1965 Ladies Singles. Roy Emerson won the Men's Singles

The prestigious Wimbledon tennis championship concluded with an Australian cleanup in the singles, after Margaret Smith defeated defending champion Maria Bueno in straight sets in the women's, and Roy Emerson beat Fred Stolle in dominant fashion in the men's. This was the first year in history that there was no British player seeded in the draw for what is frequently named *'the grandaddy of them all'* in tennis tournaments.

The first Championships were organised by the All England Croquet and Lawn Tennis Club, in 1877 and was for men only. Twenty-two players entered, providing their own racquets and shoes whilst the club's gardener provided the tennis balls with their hand-sewn flannel outer casings. As lawn tennis was a popular sport, interest in the championships grew, and by 1884, when women were finally allowed to compete, regularly drew crowds numbering 3,000. By 1900, doubles and mixed doubles matches were also a regular part of the programme, as were players from overseas, but Britain dominated the winners until 1905 when an American claimed the Women's Singles title.

Although not classed as a regular Olympic sport, it did feature in 1908 when London hosted the games and the first televised Wimbledon broadcast was made in June 1937 with the programme limited to 30 minutes. During the first world war, the championships were held as usual, but many players didn't compete either because they took active roles in combat or were prisoners of war. Two German players, being members of Kaiser Wilhelm's personal staff, were held in British prison camps for the duration of the war. However, during WW2, for six years from 1940, no tennis was played at Wimbledon. In October 1940 a bomb hit the Centre Court causing extensive damage to the stands, meaning when the Championship re-opened in 1946, fewer spectators could be accommodated.

July 9th – 15th 1965

IN THE NEWS

Friday 9 — **"Manhunt"** 150 armed police, equipped with guns, tear gas and dogs, surrounded a secluded, Surrey, country mansion in response to a tip off that escaped prisoner, Ronald Biggs, the convicted great train robber, was hiding out there. Four square miles of woodland were cornered off, but Biggs was not found.

Saturday 10 — **"Punch Card Shopping"** The first punch card shopping system in Britain appeared at a supermarket in Wallasey. Rather than picking up items, the shopper picks up a punch card instead, from there, the cards are processed by the tabulator, creating an invoice to be paid, all whilst a cashier packs the items round the back.

Sunday 11 — **"Going Over One's Head"** To meet increasing public demand over space exploration and research, the Jodrell Bank radio astronomy station is to build a £40,000 public viewing centre and exhibition hall.

Monday 12 — **"Seal Pup Hunting"** According to police reports, high velocity hunting rifles are being used to illegally hunt seal pups off the Lincolnshire coast. The hunters sell the seal skins on the open market for several pounds per kilo.

Tuesday 13 — **"Hanging Bill Abolished"** After seven months of fierce debate, The House of Commons voted to abolish capital punishment in Britain with a huge majority of 200 to 98.

Wednesday 14 — **"Fingerprint Computer"** Should ongoing tests by the joint-automatic-data-processing unit of the Home Office and Scotland Yard be successful, the fingerprints of over two million convicted criminals could be digitised for the first time.

Thursday 15 — **"Postcard from Mars"** American space probe Mariner IV sent the first ever close-up images of Mars back to earth from 135 million miles away. The painstakingly long transmission lasted 8 hours.

HERE IN BRITAIN

"Taking the Car by Train"

What appears to be the cheapest way for four people to travel from Northwest England to Scotland by train, is by taking a car, whether you plan to use it or not.

People have found that the return first class fare between Liverpool and Glasgow for an 11ft car, driver, and three passengers is only £15, whereas the return cost for four individual tickets would total £34. It With no car it costs £23 to travel third class. The trains are capable of housing 130 cars, each with an allocated luxury compartment for the driver.

AROUND THE WORLD

"Rental Canoe"

Canada's tourists can now expect an innovative service when journeying to the far North. The Hudson's Bay Company announced their new U-Paddle canoe rental service; *'the latest thing in wilderness outfitting.'*

A fraction of the cost of buying a canoe, and a world away from the birch-barked devices that immediately spring to mind, customers can expect a 17ft aluminium vessel available at various locations across the north. Much like the equivalent hire car, your U-Paddle can be picked up and dropped off at different locations.

St Swithin's Day

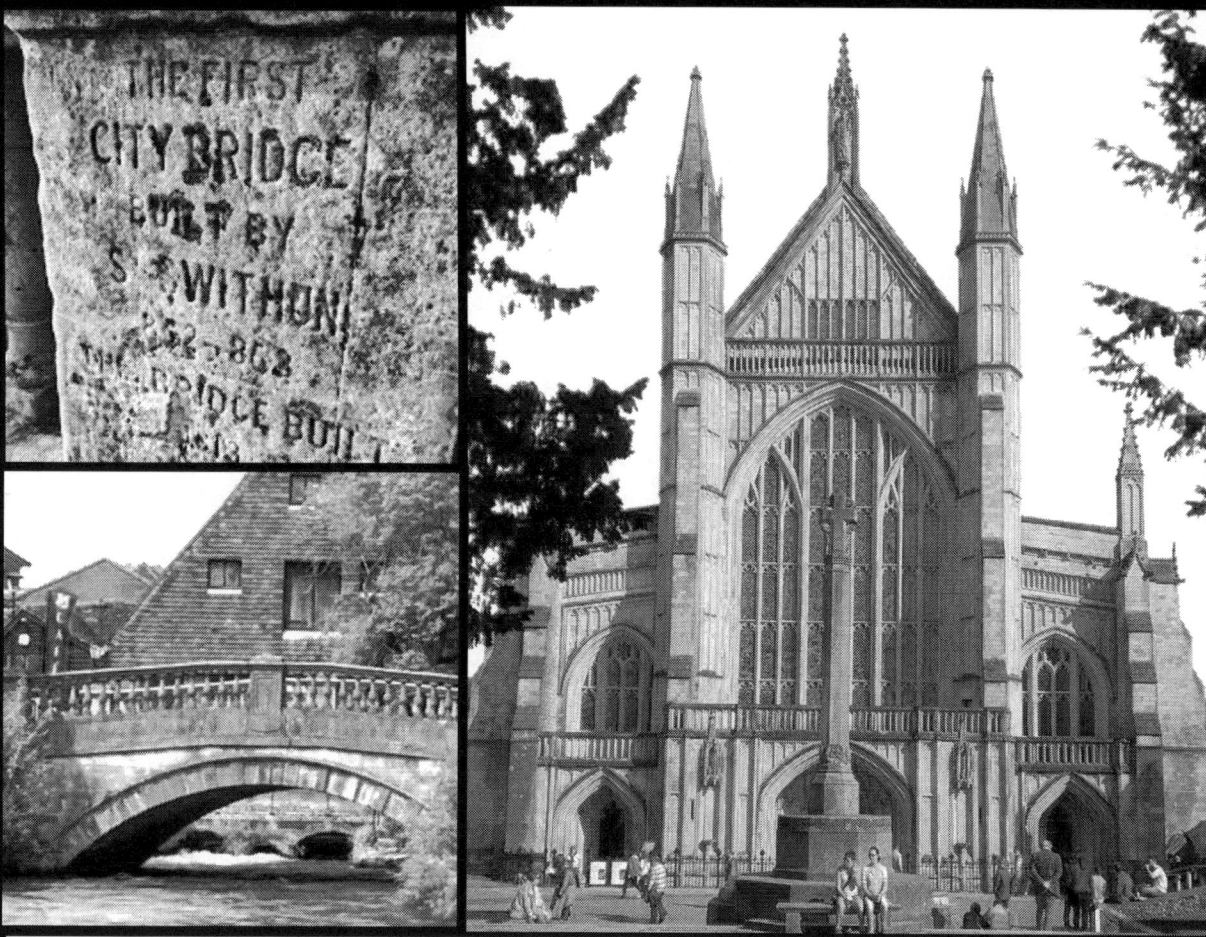

St. Swithin was an Anglo-Saxon bishop of Winchester in the 9th century. Noted for humility, he was popular with the people. On his deathbed Swithin begged to be buried outside the north wall of his cathedral, unlike other religious nobility who were buried close to the altar. He wanted to be where passers-by walked, and rain fell on it. In 971 AD, the restoration and enlargement of the building was completed, and Swithin was adopted as the cathedral's patron saint. To mark the occasion, Swithin's body was dug up and re-interred on 15th July, with much ceremony, in the new cathedral behind the altar.

Numerous miracles were reported following the move. The two most famous 'miracles' are those of the Winchester egg seller, and Queen Emma's ordeal. A woman was going to sell a basket of eggs at market. They were snatched by some workmen as a prank and got broken. In tears she prayed to St Swithin, and the eggs were 'miraculously' restored. Queen Emma, the mother of Edward the Confessor, was accused of having an affair, and to prove her innocence had to walk on red hot ploughshares. The night before her ordeal she prayed to St Swithin, and the next day was able to walk on the hot metal without injury.

According to tradition, if it rains on Saint Swithun's bridge, opposite Winchester Water Mill, on 15th July, it will rain for forty days. There is a scientific basis for this, which is that around mid-July, the jet stream settles into a pattern which holds reasonably steady until the end of August. When it lies north of Britain, continental high pressure moves in; but when it lies across or south of Britain, cooler and wetter Atlantic weather systems predominate.

July 16th – 22nd 1965

IN THE NEWS

Friday 16 — **"Super Rocket Space Station"** In a major move for space race supremacy, Russia launched a space station into orbit via a 'super rocket'. The station, called *Proton One,* is full of high-tech scientific equipment, and orbits earth once every 92.45 minutes.

Saturday 17 — **"High Security"** Following the recent escapes of three of the *'great train robbers',* the two remaining prisoners have been moved to new, high security prisons, where extra precautions will be taken to ensure their captivity.

Sunday 18 — **"Teacher's Pay Rise"** Britain's 250,000 primary and secondary school teachers were awarded a 13% pay rise, costing the government £44 million. The award raised the basic scale to £730 a year, up from £630 before.

Monday 19 — **"Glasgow Medicals"** Queues that formed over an hour and a half before opening, surprised Glasgow Corporation officials, whose free medical check-ups for men over 45 proved to be far more popular than expected.

Tuesday 20 — **"Murder Bill"** After being approved in the House of Commons last week, the House of Lords voted, by a margin of exactly 100 votes, for the Murder (Abolition of Death Penalty) Bill, officially ending capital punishment in Britain.

Wednesday 21 — **"Rhine Army Remains"** The government announced that the strength of the Rhine Army will not be severely cut unless the military as a whole is reduced. It would be more expensive to ship the troops home than to keep them there.

Thursday 22 — **"Tory Turmoil"** The former Prime Minister and Leader of the Opposition Sir Alec Douglas-Home, announced his resignation as leader of the Conservative Party. Either Edward Heath or Reginald Maudling is expected to assume the role.

HERE IN BRITAIN

"Meal-A-Minute"

A new 'meal-a-minute' drive through beside the A30 in Middlesex, confused some punters, who were unsure whether the meal was to be *prepared* or *eaten* within the minute.

The new 'fast food' scheme is set to be rolled out to the rest of the country following a successful trial; the restaurant provides meals like a one-minute cheese, onion and potato pie; spaghetti bolognaise; and chicken casserole; with the option for a hamburger in just 15 seconds for those in a real rush. *'Not quite the Savoy, but at least it's hot'* reported one customer.

AROUND THE WORLD

"Campaigning Out of Captivity"

The only killer whale in captivity, Namu, was towed 400 miles from where he was found in British Columbia, down the Pacific Coast to Seattle, where he will be 'imprisoned' in the city's aquarium. Many are not happy with the decision, not least his family, two scores of whom followed the boat transporting the four-ton whale.

Encircled by 40 of his friends and family just two hours from Port Hardy, Namu was sent into a frenzy, but after two-and-a-half hours of circling, the animals left, and Namu was taken to the aquarium without a hitch.

MONT BLANC IS OPENED

Together, President De Gaulle of France and President Saragat of Italy cut the ribbon to inaugurate the Mont Blanc Tunnel, a road that provides an impressive new link between the two countries. The seven and a quarter mile long tunnel underneath Europe's tallest mountain was a triumphant exhibition of both engineering and political brilliance.

Work began on the tunnel in 1959, when Italian engineers began tunnelling from the West, and the French from the East. Both sides were tasked with 5,800 metres of excavation, and when they finally met in the middle on September 15th, 1962, the path became the longest road tunnel in the world. The engineering mastery of the project was demonstrated when, following the final explosion linking the two sides together, it was found that the difference between the axis of the two galleries was just shy of 13 centimetres.

During construction, the teams were aided by the 100-ton machine *Jumbo,* a giant digger that could be likened to scaffolding on rails, carrying 16 perforated drills on four levels. Nearly one million cubic metres of rock was extracted from the mountain, done through 400,000 blasts powered by over 1,000 tons of explosives. The project was not without its risks; 23 men lost their lives over the four years.

The development of technology made crossing the mountain range far easier over time; the new tunnel will establish an essential inter-regional link between France and Italy, a previously treacherous and famous journey. The first recorded passage was by Hannibal Barca's Carthaginian army, when, in 218BC, 50,000 troops crossed riding elephants during their war with Rome. Further crossings were made throughout history, most notably by Napoleon, who accompanied 40,000 troops on horseback.

July 23rd – 29th 1965

IN THE NEWS

Friday 23 — **"Anti-Soviet Behaviour"** London College lecturer Gerald Brooke was sentenced to a year in gaol and four years' detention in a labour colony for *'anti-Soviet subversive activities.'* The Soviet Supreme Court delivered the ruling after Brooke was caught trying to obtain and relay information about Russia to the British embassy.

Saturday 24 — **"Double Trouble"** During a conference in London to launch a three-year public relations campaign, Chief Scout Sir Charles Maclean said that *'the Boy Scout movement should aim to double its strength within the next ten years'.*

Sunday 25 — **"123s Not ABCs"** The Postmaster General announced that, soon, telephone calls will be made solely using numbers, rather than the current letter-number hybrid system. The new scheme will introduce three-number prefixes in line with other countries.

Monday 26 — **"Maldives Independence"** The Maldives Islands are to become independent following the signing of a treaty between Britain and the Maldives Government in Colombo. Britain will keep tenure of Gan Island, which houses a strategic military base, until 1986.

Tuesday 27 — **"Ted Heath"** The Conservative Party officially chose 49-year-old Edward Heath as their new leader, after Reginald Maudling conceded following the first round of voting.

Wednesday 28 — **"Troops to Vietnam"** US President Lyndon B. Johnson committed a further 50,000 troops to Vietnam, with monthly drafts increasing from 17,000 to 35,000. This is the highest rate since the Korean War.

Thursday 29 — **"Worn Out"** Doctors complained to the Minister of Health about the dire state of the health services in Wales. There are 86 single-handed practices in Wales, tending to 2,500 patients each leaving the doctors overworked and being able to take holidays.

HERE IN BRITAIN

"As in Russia"

Former Prime Minister Harold Macmillan expressed his pleasure over the government's recent announcement that public schools were not to be abolished. He spoke of the necessity that *'the education of children should be a matter for the parent's choice, as in Russia.'*

Fee-paying schools will remain in the country, as in Russia, but only for the parents who can afford it, as in Russia. Mr Macmillan spoke of what he believes public schools to stand for, *"scholarship, service, loyalty, leadership and faith; 'exactly what this country needs.'"*

AROUND THE WORLD

"The Anastasia Case"

A former commander of Russian infantry battalions gave evidence to the Hamburg Court explicitly stating that Tsar Nicholas II and his entire family were put to death in 1918, after hearings resumed in the *Anastasia case*.

64-year-old Anna Anderson has been fighting for years for recognition that she is Grand Duchess Anastasia, the Tsar's youngest daughter, who survived the killing of her family. Countless Romanov descendants have come forward since speculation began in the 1920s, each with information changing the case.

WAR IN VIETNAM

1965 has seen a rapid increase in US Forces fighting in Vietnam. The Communist Viet Cong have taken control of much of the north and rural Vietnam. The US is desperate to prevent a Communist takeover. March saw "Operation Rolling Thunder" which bombed North Vietnam at the same time as troops attacked Viet Cong bases. The VC fought a hit and run, guerrilla style war, often blending into the local population and also developed an extensive network of tunnels, acting both as air raid shelters and safe ways of moving soldiers and equipment. Most Americans are behind the war but there are increasing protests by college students.

The war had begun in 1955 when French Indochina gained independence but split into the communist North Vietnam and US supported, democratic, South Vietnam. The North wanted to control all of Vietnam and mobilized the Viet Cong (VC), to fight a guerrilla war against the south. The US wanted to stop the spread of Communism and sent 'special advisers' to help the south, 1,000 in 1959 but 23,000 by 1964. The first 3,500 combat troops arrived in March 1965 growing to peak at 550,000 in 1973.

The persistence of the VC and growing opposition in the US, led to President Nixon withdrawing combat forces and eventually Saigon fell to the VC in 1975. In 1976 North and South Vietnam were unified under Communist rule. The human cost was massive. Between one and three million Vietnamese died and Cambodia and Laos had massive casualties. 58,200 US died, 150,00 wounded, 830,00 had PST, 50,000 deserted and 125,000 went to Canada to avoid the draft. US planes sprayed chemicals which killed 20% of the Vietnamese jungle and 33% of the mangrove forests. Chemical attacks have led to millions of injuries and deformed births. Over $1 Trillion was spent. Such costs, and no victory has influenced US foreign policy ever since, only made worse by subsequent failures in Afghanistan.

July 30th – Aug 5th 1965

IN THE NEWS

Friday 30 — **"Left to Rot"** Dockers were enraged after watching carbolic acid be poured on 5,000 cases of oranges. The fruit remained in the dock whilst their merchant struggled to find a market for them, but soon went bad; many dockers questioned why they were destroyed instead of donated to a children's home.

Saturday 31 — **"Traffic Squad"** Britain's first regional 'traffic squad' was launched in Exeter. The unit will police roads between Gloucester and Land's End in an experiment to discover the best ways of enforcing speed limits.

Sunday 1 Aug — **"World Champion"** 29-year-old Scottish sheep farmer and Lotus Formula One Team driver Jim Clark became a two-time World Champion after winning the German Grand Prix. He joins Jack Brabham as the only Brits to have won the series twice.

Monday 2 — **"Busy Getaway"** 40,000 passengers were flown out from London Airport by 500 BEA flights over the weekend. The fact that the August bank holiday now falls at the end of the month has made little difference to people's holiday plans.

Tuesday 3 — **"Clamping Down"** The Government announced tough new restrictions on immigrants from the Commonwealth with work visas to be immediately slashed from 20,800 to 8,500 per year. Until 1962, any Commonwealth citizen was free to enter the country.

Wednesday 4 — **"Amnesty for Firearms"** The Home Secretary announced an amnesty until the end of October; firearms and ammunition held illegally can be handed in to police across Britain without fear of prosecution.

Thursday 5 — **"Quiet Hospital"** The £3 million Princess Alexandra hospital in Harlow, Essex, is now complete but the wards will remain patient-less for several months, as running costs are so high that nurses cannot be afforded.

HERE IN BRITAIN

"Love 1 - Hydraulic Press 0"

A crowd of 350 journalists watched a 40-ton crusher fail to compress a 1933 Buick 'honeymoon' car. The roof was smashed by the grabber with ease, but the machine could do no more than compress the Buick into a long, sausage shaped mess.

The eight-cylinder Buick was preserved by its owner after it had taken him on a Black Forest honeymoon. It was to be crushed together with a 1932 Austin 16 and it was announced that a woman wished to use the Austin as a sentimental tombstone.

AROUND THE WORLD

"Black Sea Partying"

Holidays on the Black Sea coast are being used by Russian party goers for excessive drinking, announced the Soviet Newspaper *Trud*. Two people were recently fished out of the sea after drinking a large quantity of vodka to brace themselves for a cold plunge and another man celebrated his twenty-seventh birthday by leaping onto a restaurant table and pelting waiters with dishes, cutlery and food.

The Government is looking into ways to ensure that people behave appropriately whilst on holiday.

CIGARETTE ADVERTISING

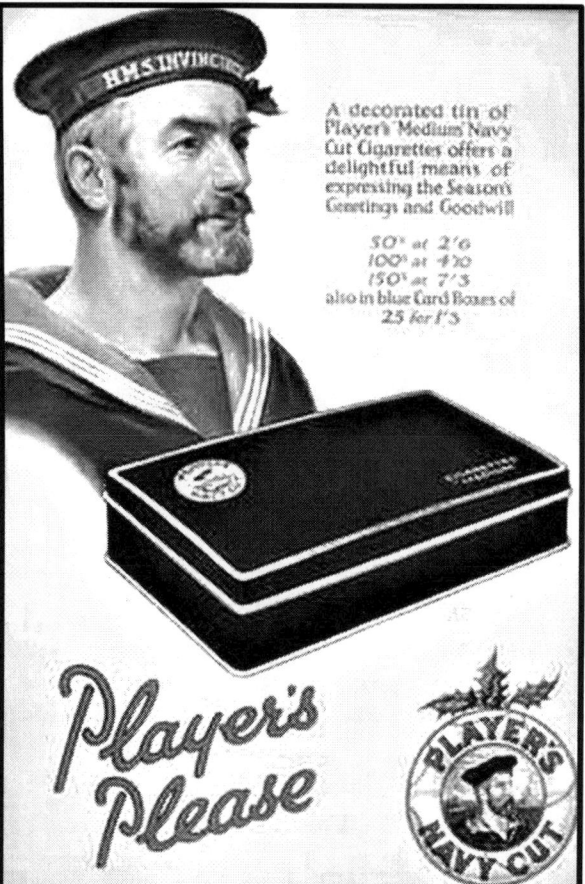

This month, cigarette advertising on television was banned in Britain, the practical ramification of the 1964 Television Act. The banning ends a long tradition of tobacco advertisement in the country, and the decision received backlash from cigarette companies and television networks alike, many of whom believe there is not sufficient evidence to prove smoking's negative health effects.

Tobacco first reached Britain in 1585, by Sir Walter Raleigh, the English explorer who was instrumental in colonising the west coast of the United States. Stories passed down, telling of a servant throwing a bucket of water over Sir Walter after seeing him smoke a pipe, fearing he was on fire. Yet, it is far more likely that tobacco existed in Britain before this point, with evidence suggesting that it was Admiral Sir John Hawkins who brought back the leaves from his overseas travels as early as 1565.

Smoking quickly gained popularity in all walks of British life, with notable critics including King James I who, in 1604, spoke of smoking being *'loathsome to the eye, hateful to the nose, harmful to the brain and dangerous to the lungs.'* As a result, he increased tobacco tax by 4,000%; but this did not deter people, many of whom believed that smoking was beneficial in protecting against ill health.

Cigarette advertisement grew rapidly throughout the 1900s. The introduction of colour lithography allowed companies to glamourise their cigarettes with colourful images and designs, and cigarette cards became a staple of everyday life until the 1940s. Cigarettes were part of army rations during both wars, endorsed by celebrities, and by 1950, 81% of men and 39% of women smoked on a regular basis. Until proper regulation was implemented last year, even doctors were being used to endorse smoking.

Aug 6th - 12th 1965

IN THE NEWS

Friday 6 — **"First Lady"** Elizabeth Lane, after becoming just the third female KC in England and the first County Court Judge, achieved further accolades by being appointed the first woman High Court Judge.

Saturday 7 — **"Casting Strike"** The strike of 80 casters at a Smethwick factory has caused more than 18,000 car workers to be laid off, costing the British Motor Corporation £5 million. The strikers decided to continue their strike, with losses to BMC set to eclipse £10 million.

Sunday 8 — **"Breaking Records"** BAE reported its largest London Airport holiday rush ever, as over 10,000 holidaymakers flew round the clock to Spain, Italy and the South of France.

Monday 9 — **"Devlin Report"** The first steps in streamlining Britain's docks took place just four days after the release of the Devlin Report, with meetings between the Government and Union leaders scheduled for this week.

Tuesday 10 — **"Royal Review"** The Queen, when reviewing the modern and versatile computer analytics of the Royal Navy Home Fleet in the Firth of Clyde, also upheld *tradition* by issuing the crew with a rum ration.

Wednesday 11 — **"Leonardo Machine"** A spinning machine designed by Leonardo Da Vinci in the 15th Century, that was never constructed, is at last being built by a small company in Lancashire. The machine solved some of the major problems that 18th Century English inventors faced when attempting to improve the spinning wheel.

Thursday 12 — **"The Medway Queen"** The Medway Queen, a steamer that brought 7,000 people back from the shores of Dunkirk in the Second World War, is again facing the threat of ship breakers because Londoners along the Thames have refused her a mooring.

HERE IN BRITAIN

"Boudica"

Boudica has been brought in to help save BOAC from financial doom. This is not the Ancient Briton Queen, but is the new automated system capable of forming world-wide electronic links and improving efficiency.

The IBM computer, costing BOAC £6 million in total, will save the company £700,000 a year in the long term. Boudica will help manage the inevitable increase in passengers over the next decade without a corresponding increase in staff and without her, they would almost certainly fall behind their competitors.

AROUND THE WORLD

"Artificial Hearts"

The National Heart Institute in Maryland USA, is developing a substitute for the human heart, a device able to function for weeks or even years. Such machines are already available, to bypass the heart and lungs during major surgery, but these are only usable for a few hours.

Six contracts have been allocated to scientific institutes across the country, and the program is aiming for success within five years. The many problems to solve include: size, power sources, reliability, pump patterns and the issue of clotting as well as making the device affordable.

Atomic Memory

Nagasaki before and after the bomb was dropped

The Enola Gay which dropped the Atom bomb over Hiroshima (below)

30,000 people gathered in Hiroshima Peace Park at 8:15am on August 6th to remember the 160,000 lives that were lost as a result of the American atomic bomb just two decades prior. Hiroshima was the first time a weapon of mass destruction was used in combat, and the subsequent attack on Nagasaki just three days later marked the last time that such a bomb was dropped. Both city centres were obliterated, but the legacy of the attacks in historical memory far eclipses the material damage.

Although the crowd was bigger than recent years, it still seemed relatively small compared to the city's now-thriving, half-a-million strong population, many of whom chose not to partake in remembrance of an event too painful to be processed. Possibly the most harrowing event of the ceremony was the placing, by the mayor, of a list of new names to be added to the death toll on the memorial. 400 people whose deaths only now can be attributed to the after-effects of the bomb, bring the total confirmed toll to 61,443. 69 of these died over the past year at the atomic bomb hospital. It is thought that as many as 160,000 people died, at least 60,000 of whom were killed by the initial blast.

Debates are ongoing about the moral and ethical implications of the bombs, with those in favour of the attacks claiming they were necessary to bring an end to the war, and the number of casualties, both civilian and military, that would have ensued from a ground invasion of Japan far outnumber the bomb's death toll. To many civil activists and social historians however, the intentional bombing of innocent civilians constitutes a war crime and were not necessary to end the war. Nevertheless, less than a week after the Nagasaki bomb, Japan surrendered to the Allies.

AUG 13TH – 19TH 1965

IN THE NEWS

Friday 13 — **"Growing Wise"** The traditional route of shoals of herring, who travel down the east coast and contribute to a large number of sales for local fisheries has changed, with herring affected by *'terrible over fishing by foreign fleets'*. The fish appeared a fortnight late, and far further South than before.

Saturday 14 — **"Call to Quit"** 3,000 doctors from Lancashire, with more than 5m patients, pledged support for the recommendation of the BMA that they should resign from the National Health Service unless the Government offer a better agreement.

Sunday 15 — **"Helicoptered In"** Prime Minister Harold Wilson cut short his Scilly Isles holiday to hold talks over Singapore's expulsion from the Federation of Malaysia last week. The meeting was held at Culdrose naval air station.

Monday 16 — **"Polio Suspects"** Four new Polio cases a day are being reported in Blackburn, as officials in the city try to contain the breakout. The number of confirmed cases is now 19.

Tuesday 17 — **"Mr Manry's Travels"** American journalist Robert Manry arrived in Falmouth aboard his 13ft boat *Tinkerbell*, having solo crossed the Atlantic Ocean. He was greeted by a flotilla of boats and hundreds of waving spectators.

Wednesday 18 — **"Television Variety"** Schedulers have been told by the Chairman of the Independent Television Authority to reduce the number of American programmes shown during the prime 8-9pm slots. It is felt that there are too many crime and western American shows at that time, and viewers would prefer more variety.

Thursday 19 — **"A Hard Day's Month"** Operation Jack Tar, which involved a convoy of the Home Fleet steaming 1,000 miles, visiting four major ports in Britain and entertaining 300,000 visitors including The Queen, has come to an end with *'unqualified success.'*

HERE IN BRITAIN

"Firearm Amnesty"

Guns galore was the headline when the Metropolitan Police showed off the spoils surrendered to them thus far in the firearm amnesty announced by the government last week. Some 450 weapons and 28,000 rounds of ammunition have been handed in to London stations, and when it closes at the end of October the number is expected to reach 3,000. This dwarfed by the 1961 amnesty, which saw 11,000 weapons surrendered, one of which was by a man who brought a live hand grenade he had been using for some time as a door stop.

AROUND THE WORLD

"Cushioning the Blow"

Warnings to spectators in four languages echoed throughout the bull-fighting ring in Costa Brava cautioning the public against throwing cushions into the arena.
Prohibitions were read in Spanish, English, French and German making it clear that it was not okay for bull fighting aficionados to throw cushions, supplied to cover the arena's cement seats, into the ring when they are not happy with the performance of a matador. Punishments could include fines and even arrest.

Unlucky For Some!

This ship has no deck 13.

When a woman called Melbourne dockers out on strike, having telephoned to dock 13 on Friday the thirteenth and said the waterside workers' federal council was ordering the men to cease work immediately, five gangs working on the British ship Braeside stopped work and went home. They should have guessed something was wrong. For many, Friday 13th which occurs one to three times per year is regarded as the most unlucky day of the year. Superstitions surrounding the date are thought to originate in the middle-ages and there are dozens of fears, myths and old wives' tales associated with the date all over the world. Some people even suffer from Triskaidekaphobia, the fear or avoidance of the number 13 or 'Paraskevidekatriaphobia', the crippling fear of Friday the 13th.

The number 13 and Friday both have an individual long history of bringing bad luck. In the Bible, Judas, who betrayed Jesus, was the 13th guest to sit down to the Last Supper. In Norse mythology, a dinner party of the gods was ruined by the 13th guest called Loki, 'god of deceit and evil', who caused the world to be plunged into darkness. Peoples of the Mediterranean, regarded 13 with suspicion, not being as perfect as 12, which is divisible in many ways.

As for 'Friday', according to tradition, Adam and Eve were expelled from Eden; Cain murdered Abel; St John the Baptist was beheaded the enactment of the order of Herod for the massacre of the innocents, all took place on a Friday. In Chaucer's Canterbury Tales, written in the 14th Century, he says 'and on a Friday fell all this mischance'. Here in Britain, Friday was once known as 'Hangman's Day' because it was usually when people who had been condemned to death would be hanged and the great crash of 1869, when the price of gold plummeted, was on Friday too.

Aug 20th – 26th 1965

IN THE NEWS

Friday 20 — **"Four Day Week"** 10,000 Ford Motor Company workers will be reduced to a four-day week following the government's latest tightening of financial restrictions. Home market demand over the last six months has dropped dramatically.

Saturday 21 — **"Tapped Calls"** Post Office officials investigated allegations by a weekly newspaper, the Wiltshire Echo, that telephone calls are *'frequently and consistently tapped'* at the Chippenham exchange. The paper's owner, the Labour MP for Bosworth, reported that even calls by members of the Royal Family are listened to.

Sunday 22 — **"Tea Only for Prisoners"** Cocoa has been removed from prison diet sheets, with inmates now being offered only tea; when current supplies run out, prisoners will get half a pint of tea with dinner and, for inmates under 21, during morning exercise.

Monday 23 — **"Floating Village"** The residents of London's 'floating village', a yacht basin in Chiswick, are opposing the plans of a development company to fill the basin and build luxury flats. The basin has been used for residential mooring of 50 boats since 1920.

Tuesday 24 — **"Liner Train"** British Railways' £100 million 'liner train' scheme for express freight travel is under threat, after the Executive of the National Union of Railwaymen refused to cooperate with the implementation.

Wednesday 25 — **"Scottish Plant"** The largest private investment into Scottish infrastructure has been pledged, with Imperial Chemical Industries' new £31 million factory in Ayrshire. The plant will employ over 1,000 people.

Thursday 26 — **"Fishy Business"** HMS Letterson, the UK's fishery protection ship, intervened after 26 Russian and over 200 Dutch and German trawlers fishing in our waters off the Yorkshire coast. Of 115 ships visible from a Whitby cliff top, just 25 were British.

HERE IN BRITAIN

"Scouts Strike Gold"

A group of 30 Scouts struck gold whilst mining in the hills of north Wales. The London Scouts were on a 14-day summer camp exploring and working a derelict mine near Dolgellau when they stumbled across the valuable material.

As it stands, the boys have retrieved half an ounce, worth about £6, though the group scout master has said *'the aim is to find enough gold to pay for the trip.'* The target certainly looks possible, as the scouts, equipped with pickaxes and miners' helmets, have been hard at work, incentivised by their discovery.

AROUND THE WORLD

"Stuck in Time"

A time capsule has been lowered 15 yards into the ground just 10 feet away from a similar box from 1939, marking the end of the New York World's Fair on its penultimate day.

Inside, 117,000 pages of microfilmed records from between 1940 and 1965, along with 45 other objects including credit cards, a bikini, birth control pills, filter cigarettes, a heat shield from Apollo 7, and photographs and books from some of America's finest actors, poets and artists. The boxes are not to be opened before the year 6939AD.

Edinburgh Tattoo

Over a quarter of a million people attended the first night of the Edinburgh Military Tattoo in the grounds of the floodlit Edinburgh castle, where they watched Royal Marine commandos perform alongside James Bond, Goldfinger and Oddjob. The five-minute item was not without drama however, as two women and a man were injured after Bond's famous Aston Martin DB5 skidded into spectators during one of the stunts. Nevertheless, the act was retained for the rest of the festival, and still received a great reception from the public.

As always, the military tattoo was the most popular of the whole event, and the year-round bitter winds on the top of the cliff failed to deter spectators, who flocked throughout August and September to watch commandos climb the castle walls, perform field gun manoeuvres, and give a top-quality military display. This year saw the inaugural performance from members of the Fijian Military, who dazzled the crowds with aboriginal dance and music, wearing garments almost inseparable from a kilt; as the festival endured, it became clear that Fijians and Scots had far more in common than expected, not least in their choice of clothing.

The Edinburgh Tattoo has been ingrained in British tradition since its inaugural staging in 1950. Its humble beginnings were inspired by a 1949 Ross Bandstand performance of a play called *'Something About a Soldier'* for the Edinburgh International Festival of Music and Drama. The play was such a hit that the Lieutenant responsible was invited the following year to present a whole military show, an eight-act strong event in 1950. Since then, the festival has grown exponentially: in 1952 the first overseas performers came over, and in 1953 the first women's group took part; in total over 50 nations have participated in what is now a truly international spectacle.

Aug 27th – Sept 2nd 1965

IN THE NEWS

Friday 27 — **"Spending a Penny Strike"** Workers at the British Motor Corporation lay idle for the second time in three weeks in protest against the sacking of a female machinist at a felt mill in Coventry for *'spending too long on the toilet.'*

Saturday 28 — **"Drivers' Strike"** The Ford car factory in Halewood, Liverpool, ended its last production shift for 12 days, after a strike of 300 externally-employed delivery drivers halted distribution. By the morning, all available factory space was occupied by 8,000 new cars.

Sunday 29 — **"Space Triumph"** After eight days and 120 rotations in orbit, the US Gemini V spacecraft safely returned to earth. Both astronauts were in good spirits when picked up by helicopter from their landing spot in the Atlantic.

Monday 30 — **"Atheistic Counselling"** Pastoral care for 'unbelievers' will be provided in an experimental scheme by the British Humanist Association. 'Counsellors' will fulfil many of the roles of a Parish priest, advising on social questions and problems of disbelief.

Tuesday 31 — **"Lessons By TV"** 300 lessons by television will be distributed across 315 schools and colleges in Glasgow to help take stress off teachers in the area. The £50,000 per-year system already has recorded programmes on French, geometry and algebra.

Wed 1 Sept — **"Radioactive"** Preventative measures are being taken in the Holy Loch American Polaris submarines base, after an increase in radioactivity, caused by the discharge of coolants from the submarine reactor plants was reported by monitoring stations.

Thursday 2 — **"Europa 1"** The test launch of Europe's first space satellite launcher *Europa 1*, failed for the second time in a fortnight following an engine failure. There will be no third test for at least a week.

HERE IN BRITAIN

"August Bank Holiday"

The second day of the experimental 'end of the month August Bank holiday' began quieter than expected, with the RAC describing it as *'half-hearted';* clearly something of a 'don't speak too soon' moment, as chaos ensued on the roads after 7pm, when the homeward journey from coastal resorts began.

Whilst traffic was *'heavy but orderly'* in many places, some areas faced *'a see-saw Sunday'*, and police broke up a number of fights between Mods and Rockers in Brighton, though once again, comparatively fewer than previous Bank holidays.

AROUND THE WORLD

"Beating the Draft"

Large numbers of young American men were hastily married before midnight on August 27th, in an attempt to *'beat the draft'*. President Johnson's announcement that men between the ages of 19 and 26 who got married after August 27th were to be liable for military service clearly incentivised a number of couples to rapidly 'tie the knot', with most of the ceremonies held in Nevada and Arizona.

In Las Vegas, 114 licenses were given out in the two hours before midnight, and Nevada was popular because it imposes no blood tests or waiting period.

Trains Without A Name

Many of the well-known 'expresses' between London, Wales and the West Country will run from Paddington without the names that helped make them famous. The now nameless lines include, the *Bristolian,* the *Mayflower,* the *Royal Duchy* and the Capital's *United Express*, all staunchly recognisable from their great name placards. Western Region Rail has explained the unpopular move as *'a sacrifice on the altar of progress',* as often these great trains lay idle for several hours in between their runs up and down the country. Given the drive for maximum use of equipment, this process is no longer viable and henceforth, trains will be turned around in a matter of minutes, to be sent off to different destinations. The constant placement and removal of name boards would be *'impracticable'.* However, this is far from the end of named trains, as Western Rail *'recognise them to be part of the glamour of the railways';* many of the best known names will still make the journeys emblazoned with their insignias: the *Cornish Riviera Express,* the *Torbay Express,* the *Devonian,* the *Cornishman,* and the *Cheltenham Spa Express* are all routes where there is no opportunity for additional use, and can remain as rail travellers favourites.

It was Britain who pioneered inter-city rail travel as early as 1830, when the Liverpool to Manchester railway opened, the first of its kind anywhere in the world. By 1850, Britain had the most advanced rail network in the world, with other European nations seeking British expertise in design and execution. And yet, by the 1950s, following an era of diesel and electric implementation, British Rail were fighting with the ever-growing motoring industry. This ultimately culminated in major reductions in the network by 1965, with *The Beeching Axe* forcing the closure of over a third of stations deemed to be 'uneconomic'.

SEPT 3RD – 9TH 1965

IN THE NEWS

Friday 3 — **"Tried for Size"** A British Railways liner train was 'tried for size' at a specially built depot in Manchester after making the journey up from London. The 1,000ft long train will remain in the terminal overnight for members of the NUR to inspect.

Saturday 4 — **"Ultimatum on Strikes"** The Government told the motor industry that they will be forced to intervene unless car companies work out a way to deal with the flood of unofficial strikes damaging the industry.

Sunday 5 — **"Schweitzer's Funeral"** Dr Albert Schweitzer, the *Saint of the Jungle,* was buried before mourning Africans in the grounds of the jungle hospital in which he worked for fifty years.

Monday 6 — **"Ford Factory at Work"** After striking for nearly three weeks, 300 delivery drivers began to work through the 8,000 strong backlog of Ford cars parked outside the factory in Liverpool. The cars should be cleared by the end of the month and production in the factory has resumed.

Tuesday 7 — **"Channel Relay"** The Wembley-based Phoenicians Swimming Club completed a world record relay swim from France to England in a time of 9 hours and 58 minutes. The previous record was over 10 hours, set by a Middlesbrough team last June.

Wednesday 8 — **"Police Complaints"** No changes are to be made to 150,000 already-circulated Home Office leaflets advising the public how to complain against the police; however, the force is prepared to adapt the pamphlets should they lead to *'frivolous complaints'*.

Thursday 9 — **"Wilson's Ban on Weapons"** The Prime Minister announced that Britain will halt all arms shipments to India until a United Nations update on the situation in Pakistan. Earlier this month, India invaded West Pakistan.

HERE IN BRITAIN

"The Lord's Lions' Den"

Lord Bath has obtained planning permission from the Wiltshire County Council for the building of a 12ft high fence around part of his estate in Longleat. The 100-acre enclosure will be used to keep his Lordship's collection of 50 live lions, and he plans to allow visitors to drive through for a small cost.

Although the permission could be revoked by the Minister of Housing, Wiltshire Council have no plans to go back on their decision; Lord Bath said, *'there is no law in England forbidding me from keeping a lion where I want to.'*

AROUND THE WORLD

"Toy Bomb"

An American spokesperson in South Vietnam announced that US forces will make air drops of sweets and toys over communist controlled North Vietnam. These new *'joy'* raids are the brainchild of US psychologists and are intended to contrast dramatically with the daily air attacks on strategic and military positions.

This 'battle of the minds' with gestures of friendship to the North Vietnamese people might counter the stream of anti-American propaganda being circulated in the area and show them that the South's standard of living is not as low as 'they are told it is.'

Saint Of The Jungle

The pioneering medical missionary to Africa

Hospital workers and lepers paid their respects to the late Dr Albert Schweitzer in a touching ceremony in Lambarene, the Capital city of Gabon, on the grounds of the hospital in which he worked for over 50 years. His grave was marked with a homemade wooden cross, and the daily running of his hospital has been handed over to his daughter. Although the ceremony was modest, international recognition flooded the hospital from world leaders; the Queen was first to pay her respects in a letter to Dr Schweitzer's only daughter, Mime, and others soon followed from US President Johnson, the West German Chancellor, the Presidents of Italy and France, and even a message from Moscow.

Lambarene was where Dr Schweitzer chose to die, having made a powerful statement to doctors on his ninetieth birthday in January, *'I feel at home here and belong to you until my dying breath'* and the President of Gabon assured his people that the Doctor's *'life work and human fraternity will be continued'* long after his death.

Dr Schweitzer first visited Lambarene as a medical missionary at the beginning of the century and, after qualifying as a doctor in Hamburg in 1913, he returned and founded his hospital. After a brief period in a French concentration camp in 1917, Dr Schweitzer spent the rest of his life helping those in need in Gabon, with many travelling hundreds of miles to receive treatment. Soon Schweitzer was wholly ingrained in city life; not only was he a doctor and surgeon at his own hospital, but he was also a pastor of a congregation, administrator of a village, superintendent of buildings, a writer of scholarly books, a musician and a gracious host. There was not a pursuit of Gabonian life in which Dr Schweitzer was not involved.

Sept 10th – 16th 1965

IN THE NEWS

Friday 10 — **"Teething Troubles"** The 12,000 NHS dentists in Britain will get an extra shilling (5p) for every patient's mouth examined following changes to their pay structure. This provides dentists with an incentive to see more patients and to give a significant pay increase

Saturday 11 — **"Recruitment Drive"** Plaid Cymru, the Welsh Nationalist Party, launched a recruitment drive coinciding with their first televised political broadcast. The drive, *'larger than any campaign of its kind'*, has already seen hundreds of members sign up.

Sunday 12 — **"Bowmen of Mercy"** A herd of deer will be hunted down by bow and arrow to save their lives, as their current estate in Shropshire becomes a farm. The arrows will be tranquilliser darts, and the animals will be rehomed 100 miles away in Scunthorpe Nature Park, Lincolnshire.

Monday 13 — **"Potty Mouth"** Manchester United Football Club banned eight young fans until the end of the season for chanting swear words at a referee in the club's home match against Stoke City.

Tuesday 14 — **"Work Shy"** The Chairman of the National Coal Board disputed newspapers' claims that 'miners' failure to turn up to work in recent months', was the sole reason for the closure of six coal pits in South Wales.

Wednesday 15 — **"Commonwealth Arts Festival"** An American woman, thrilled by her first ride on an open top double decker bus, was one of the 50,000 people in Hyde Park who watched a £3,000 firework display at the opening ceremony of the inaugural Commonwealth Arts Festival.

Thursday 16 — **"Germ-Trap Knife"** A prisoner smuggled a *'filthy germ trap'* tin knife out of Brixton prison and showed it to his local MP, who was so shocked, he appealed to the Home Office and managed to get them banned.

HERE IN BRITAIN

"Crack-ing Down"

The ten companies given exclusive licences to break second quality eggs may have to pay more than £300,000 to the Egg Marketing Board. All eggs with hairline cracks and other faults deeming them not good enough for shelves are broken for the liquid market.

These 'second quality eggs' make up 1.4 million of the 22 million eggs sold in Britain annually. When the scheme was introduced last year, many smaller companies complained that the exclusive licences afforded some farms excessive profits.

AROUND THE WORLD

"Hurricane Betsy"

Over 150 people died in the New Orleans area after Hurricane Betsy struck this week. There has been a particularly sharp demand for snakebite serum. Large numbers of poisonous snakes have been forced out of their usual hiding places by the floods.

Also enough poison to kill 40,000 people menaced part of Louisiana after a barge loaded with 600 tons of liquid chlorine disappeared during the storm in the Mississippi near the state capital of Baton Rouge.

COLCHESTER OYSTERS

The River Colne Near Colchester

At the traditional opening of the oyster fishery off Brightlingsea, for the first time in two years, the official dredge revealed good quality top-size oysters in the famous Pyefleet beds. The first Colchester native oysters of the new season were dredged and eaten in their bed in the Pyefleet Creek onboard the fisheries vessel 'Crocus'.

The burgesses of Colchester have held the right to fish the Colne for oysters 'from time beyond which memory runneth not to the contrary' and it fell to the mayor, Councillor Stanley Wooster, to lower the first dredge. Meanwhile, the Town Clerk had read to the corporation and the fishermen who had gathered, the proclamation first made on this same water in 1256, whereby *'our very excellent Lord King' Henry III confirmed the burgesses in their right and forbade poaching under pain of forfeiture and grievous amercements.'* In Tudor times, Colchester 'natives' were given as gifts from the local authority to the Sovereign or their Courtiers if they visited the town, often allowing the Borough benefits in return and up to the start of the Great War, the Natives appeared on the tables of the rich and powerful across the world.

The party later adjourned to the Anchor, where with three cheers for the Queen, the traditional toast of gin with gingerbread was taken. Colchester oysters may be back on the market soon but a drop in orders from London west end restaurants for the larger, grade one, natives, which sold for between 30s and 35s is causing concern. The reason is believed to be the decline in business entertaining since the Budget changes affecting expense-account meals. The more select restaurants, where the charge was around £5 or £6 for a meal, seem to have been the hardest hit.

SEPT 17TH – 23RD 1965

IN THE NEWS

Friday 17 — **"Anti-Traffic Clubs"** Brighton has become the first British city to enforce licences for the city's coffee bars and clubs, in a bid to help police against teenage drug trafficking. As it stands, the town's institutions are *'a danger to the youth of today.'*

Saturday 18 — **"Commonwealth Immigration"** The Archbishop of Canterbury will head the new National Committee for Commonwealth Immigrants to *'promote and coordinate the integration of Commonwealth immigrants into the community.'*

Sunday 19 — **"The Damn French"** The sight of a Tricolore flying over a parish church in Yarmouth, Isle of Wight, sparked uproar amongst residents. Those educated in the area's local history told of the French ransacking the town in 1377 and 1524. The flag was hoisted by the Reverend, who married a Parisian couple there.

Monday 20 — **"Soviet Good Will"** The first Russian ship to sail down the Thames since before the war dropped anchor opposite the Tower of London. The oceanographic vessel *Nikolai Zubov* came to Britain on a goodwill visit.

Tuesday 21 — **"Sea Gem"** British Petroleum struck gas several thousand feet below sea level on their *Sea Gem* rig in the North Sea. Current data suggests that there is not yet a sufficient volume to be deemed commercially significant.

Wednesday 22 — **"A Cracking Start"** Several hairline cracks have appeared in the welding of HMS Dreadnought, the Royal Navy's first atomic submarine; the vessel's scheduled re-fit has been brought forward as a top priority.

Thursday 23 — **"Bart's Staff in Revolt"** As many as 80 doctors at St Bartholomew's Hospital London have complained about their salaries and working conditions, with many threatening to leave the country for America. The current NHS provisions cannot sustain workers' families.

HERE IN BRITAIN
"Hidden Treasure"

Demolition men knocking down a 14-room mansion in Edgbaston, Birmingham, stumbled across the contents of a house that had been left untouched for 31 years. The men found the house furnished exactly as when it was last occupied in 1934; a copy of *Punch* from 1924 still sat on the coffee table, cobwebs eerily covered family photographs, and in the kitchen, bottles of jam still lined the shelves.

According to rumour, the house had been abandoned since the young girl who lived there was left at the altar, the owner died a spinster.

AROUND THE WORLD
"The Sydney Opera House"

A British opera producer has described Sydney's £24 million opera-house project as *'a joke ... actually hilarious would be the better word.'* He, like many others, is not a fan of the new building, with many leading figures in opera weighing in on the size, look and feel of the place.

'It will prove to be the greatest white elephant of the century' said one pundit, with another commenting that it would take *'a man of genius'* to run the building. Many have predicted much difficulty in ticket sales due to the building's *'ugly'* nature.

Battle Of Britain Celebrations

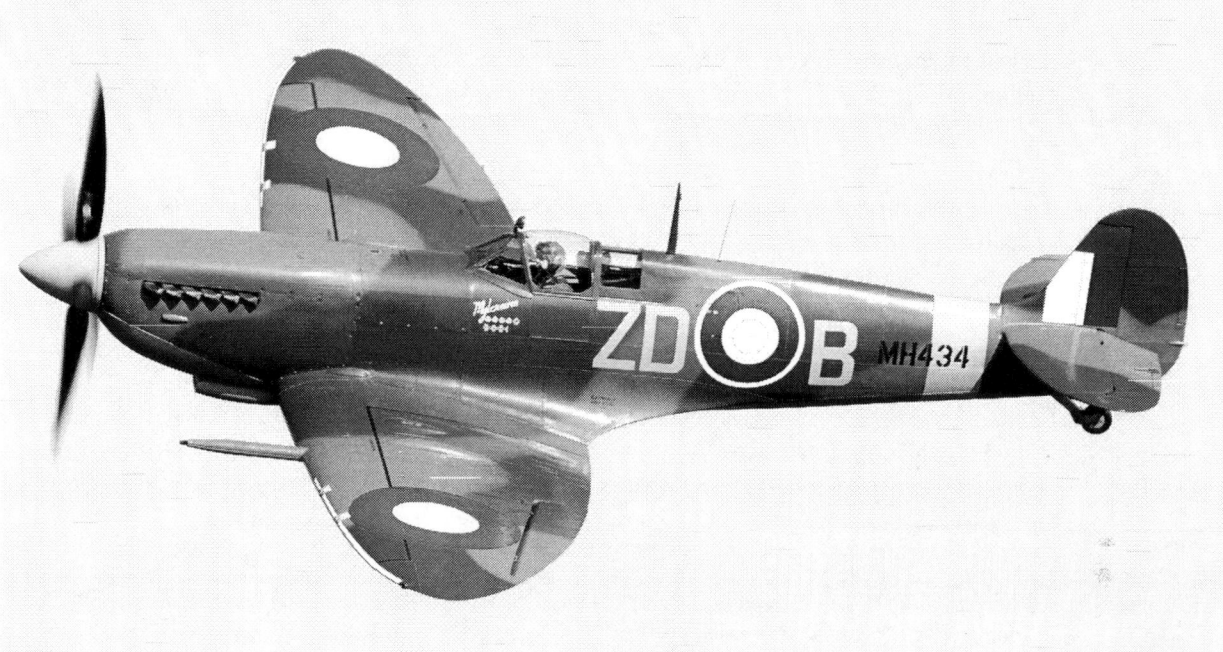

The RAF Spitfire

Celebrations up and down the country marked the twenty-fifth anniversary of the Battle of Britain. A ceremony at Westminster Abbey saw the Queen unveil a commemorative plaque to the late Sir Winston Churchill, who died earlier this year, and at noon a Spitfire and a Hurricane flew in formation over the wartime Prime Minister's grave in Bladon churchyard.

When the war of 1914 started, the aeroplane was a new and untried weapon, strictly limited in its uses and not sure of its role. Rapidly it developed both as a weapon of offence and defence. When the allies mounted their counter-offensive in 1918, the RAF was able to concentrate 1,290 first-line aircraft against its opponents' 340, and, enjoying this air superiority, was able to disrupt the Germans' communications and harass their troops through low flying attacks. When the Armistice came, the RAF was the greatest air force in the world, both numerically and in quality of equipment, possessing more than 200 squadrons, 22,647 aircraft, 103 airships and a total strength of 291,000 officers and men. After the war the Service shrank to a shadow of its former self but managed to keep many members possessing a pioneering spirit, which in turn, maintained the high standards and increased the prestige of British aviation throughout the world.

At the beginning of the Second World War, Britain had far fewer planes than Germany, forcing the country to undergo a massive drive to build Spitfires and Hurricane fighters, and Wellington, Whitley and Hampden bombers. During the summer of 1940, the RAF fended off daily campaigns by the German Luftwaffe to destroy our southernmost airbases, with large degrees of success. Although technically superior to the German planes, the RAF's Spitfire and Hurricane aircraft were heavily numerically outnumbered, it was a dangerous situation until the Battle of Britain had been won.

SEPT 24TH - 30TH 1965

IN THE NEWS

Friday 24 — **"Cigar Demand"** A cigarette factory in Ipswich, Suffolk, has been converted in a £1.5M scheme to meet the growing demand for cigars which rose 34 percent just last year.

Saturday 25 — **"Match of the Day"** After patching up their four-month row with the Football Association over TV Football, the BBC's *Match of the Day* returned to TV screens, with 45 minutes of highlights from the week's matches.

Sunday 26 — **"A Gypsy Welcome"** The Pope chose to spend his sixty-eighth birthday amongst a camp of 3,000 gypsies outside Rome. The religious encampment represents the first international pilgrimage to be undertaken by Roman Catholic gypsies to the Pontiff.

Monday 27 — **"Blue Streak Lives"** The Minister of Aviation refuted recent rumours by confirming that Britain's *Blue Streak* rocket programme is not to be scrapped. The Minister assured workers in a speech at the rocket launch site in Gilsland, Cumberland.

Tuesday 28 — **"Ladies Day"** Maria Atanassova became the first woman to captain a commercial aircraft landing at Heathrow. The Bulgarian pilot for the airline *Tabso* landed a Russian aircraft carrying 73 passengers.

Wednesday 29 — **"Michaelmas Day Dedication"** A Church built by parishioners in their spare time at Hellesdon, Norfolk, for the price of £3,300, was dedicated by the Bishop of Norwich. The DIY church was built with a minimum of professional help.

Thursday 30 — **"Doctors vs NHS"** The possibility of an alternative, old fashioned, family doctor service to rival the National Health Service is gaining more traction amongst doctors, with 23,000 medical professionals pledging money towards the scheme. The project intends to supply healthcare to households for a weekly premium of 2s 9d (14p) per week.

HERE IN BRITAIN

"Rain Kills Plaice"

Over 200,000 of the plaice released into a Scottish sea loch during a fish farming experiment last August, have died. The mortality rate was higher than 75%, with heavy rain, contaminated and desalinated water lowering oxygen levels, and decaying organic matter all contributing to the animals' deaths.

Further hazards include the invasion of predators like crabs and eels, who prey on the small plaice, predators whom the authorities have assured will be controlled more effectively in the future.

AROUND THE WORLD

"Breaking the Constitution"

The British High Commissioner of Aden, after suspending the constitution due to increased security issues, set up a government to help maintain direct control of the state. Aden has been plagued by mounting terrorism and riots, which has forced the British government to revoke the city's self-rule status.

British run schools were shut, bars and cinemas were declared out of bounds to British servicemen and the curfew was extended amidst ever-growing gunfire incidents.

The Grocers' Company

A fire caused irreparable damage to *Grocers Hall* on Prince Street in London. The home to the *Grocers' Company,* one of the few remaining livery halls in the Capital to have survived the bombing of the Second World War, was *'reduced to shell'*, with the fire severely damaging the library, offices, banqueting hall and livery hall of the building. The *Worshipful Company of Grocers* is one of the City of London's 'great twelve' Livery Companies, ranking second in their order of precedence. The age of the guild cannot be overstated; they formed as early as 1180, under the name of *'Pepperers',* whose role it was to prevent the contamination of spices and drugs. Soon their role expanded into wider merchandise, resulting in their name change to *'Grosseurs',* in the 1370s. It was in 1425 that the Grocers bought the hall on Prince Street.

The title of a 'LIvery company', dates back to as early as the first guilds in the 12th Century. As society developed, and the earliest forms of British capitalism grew in fruition, these guilds became more individualised, often characterising themselves by specific clothes, or 'liveries', to distinguish themselves from other guilds. By the 14th Century, there were 48 well-established companies that had earned political influence with the Lord Mayor through charters and ordinances. Now, livery companies are one of the cornerstones for political operation in London, responsible for the election of Sheriffs of the City of London and hold large influence with the mayor. Many livery companies still support various alms-houses across the country and sit on a dedicated committee, helping to seek joint initiatives for the future; in essence, the livery companies control much of London both politically and financially, and often work together across multiple industries to foster support for their own interests.

Oct 1st – Oct 7th 1965

IN THE NEWS

Friday 1 — **"Barrage Building"** Eel fisheries could take over from shrimp and cockles should the proposed barrage be built in Morecombe Bay. The barrage would encourage the nesting of birds, meaning that the crustaceans would disappear from the area.

Saturday 2 — **"The Great Hunt"** The Government's £80 million search for gas below the North Sea has paid off; British Petroleum became the first company to strike gas in the area, some 800ft below sea level.

Sunday 3 — **"Secret Meetings"** Ian Smith, the Prime Minister of Rhodesia, left for London to engage in talks with the British Government over terms of independence. The plans were kept secret, and the PM was picked up in an unmarked airliner diverted from Johannesburg.

Monday 4 — **"Extra-Curricular Activity"** Members of the National Association of Schoolmasters began their ban on duties outside of school hours, including the marking of work, the running of clubs, and the supervision of sport, following disappointment over recent pay awards.

Tuesday 5 — **"Collect Your Own"** British Railways' parcel distribution system at King's Cross descended into such chaos that the company invited disgruntled customers, waiting up to three weeks for their parcel, to *'collect their own.'* Packages stacked high on trailers stretched for 100 yards along platform one.

Wednesday 6 — **"Closed Circuit Victory"** Although their team lost 3-1 against Cardiff, supporters of Coventry City were in high spirits watching the first closed circuit broadcast of a game of British football on a 40ft x 30ft television screen.

Thursday 7 — **"Robot Postman"** The Post Office *'poised for a plunge into automation'* displayed some of their new 'robot postmen' at an exhibition in London. The machines can read and sort 20,000 letters per hour.

HERE IN BRITAIN

"Land of Beauty and Usefulness"

The *'ugliness'* of derelict brick works in and around Peterborough will undergo a transformation project to restore the area to *'a land of beauty and usefulness'*. Over 2,000 acres of waterlogged, abandoned brick clay excavations will be filled in with 30 million tons of ash from the Trent Valley power stations.

The ash will be pulverised into a substance *'as finely ground as face powder'*, known as P.F.A, before being mixed with water and pumped as sludge into the clay pits at a rate of 10,000 tons of ash a day.

AROUND THE WORLD

"October Revolution II"

Sweden embarked on their second *'October Revolution'* in drinking allowance. The country abolished the restriction of only three litres of strong liquor every month per adult and then has just increased the strength of beer permitted from 2.8% to 3.6%.

Vast quantities of beer was rushed to Sweden by ship from Britain, Germany, Denmark and Holland to take advantage of this sudden new market, with more than 50 million bottles arriving on the first day.

Constable Of The Tower

The Constable of the Tower of London and the ceremonial gold key.

Field-Marshal Sir Gerald Templer, the new Constable of the Tower of London was installed this week in a ceremony that reaches back almost 900 years. About 20 Yeoman Warders formed a circle on the grass, dressed in scarlet and gold with tricolour rosettes and ribbons. In the centre stood the Chief Warder and near him the Yeoman Gaoler carried the gleaming processional axe. The Lord Chamberlain came out from the King's House carrying a ceremonial gold key on a red velvet cushion. Behind him walked in procession the new Constable, the Lieutenant of the Tower and the Resident Governor and Major of the Tower. The band struck up a Royal Salute in honour of the Queen's representative, who had come *'in the Queen's name and on Her Majesty's behalf, to deliver the Keep and Custody of Her Majesty's Palace and Fortress of the Tower.'*

The role was established by William the Conqueror around 1078 and the holder was then known as the Keeper of the Tower and historically, he controlled the operation, upkeep and security of the Tower and everyone who lived and worked within it. He was also responsible for the Tower's, often famous, prisoners. In return for his service, the Constable was given the right to seize any swan that swam under London Bridge; any horse, ox, cow, pig or sheep that fell into the Thames from the bridge and any cart that fell into the Tower of London's moat. Every ship that came upstream to the city had to moor at Tower Wharf to unload a portion of its cargo for the Constable and although the role is largely ceremonial today, this tradition is still upheld at the annual Ceremony of the Constable's Dues. When a ship of the Royal Navy visits the Port of London, the Captain presents a barrel of wine, his 'Dues', to the Constable on Tower Green.

Oct 8th – 14th 1965

IN THE NEWS

Friday 8 — **"Post Office Tower"** A new stamp was issued to mark the opening of the tallest building in Britain, London's 620ft Post Office Tower. The building is easily visible in amongst the Georgian-architecture of Fitzrovia.

Saturday 9 — **"Mammoth's Tooth"** An amateur geologist in Oxford, made the discovery of his life when he stumbled across the lower molar of a 150,000-year-old curly-tusked woolly mammoth. The man described his assessment of the tooth so accurately that the British museum immediately dispatched someone to verify the discovery.

Sunday 10 — **"London Stansted"** Objections to the Government's proposal to develop Stansted Airport in Essex into a third London international airport will be heard at an independent public enquiry. The aviation minister affirmed that this was a question of suitability of location, rather than requirements for the additional airport.

Monday 11 — **"Going It Alone"** The Rhodesian Prime Minister announced in a statement as he left London, that *'the talking is over'* in independence negotiations with the British Government, and that a *'go-it-alone'* declaration is the only avenue remaining.

Tuesday 12 — **"Technicians Strike"** In what was deemed the first national strike by university staff, 95% of all institution's technicians refused to work for one-day, marching through streets carrying placards demanding increased pay and status.

Wednesday 13 — **"Forcing the Hand"** £546 million worth of work in hand in architects' offices has been abandoned following the Chancellor's recent construction restrictions.

Thursday 14 — **"Striking Gold"** The National Coal Board drilling tower, after seven years has struck an additional 550 million tons worth of coal, worth £2.5 billion. The tower, digging its eighteenth and final bore hole off the coast of Durham, employs 20,000 workers.

HERE IN BRITAIN
"Automated Teller Machine"

Automated cash dispensing machines, available 24 hours a day, every day, are under consideration by at least one major bank. The system, named the *Automated Teller Machine* (ATM) is set to solve the problems of Saturday opening hours and round-the-clock facilities without increasing the burden on staff.

Built into the outside walls of branches, the machines would issue limited amounts of money when fed with a scannable voucher by a customer. Although the scheme would cost the banks upwards of £7 million, the justification of improved service seems credible.

AROUND THE WORLD
"British Week in Milan"

Milan's streets were ablaze with Union Jacks as the city opened its *'British Week'*, showcasing the best of British exports. British policemen attracted large crowds, whether 'on duty', courtesy of Milan's local authorities, or taking a break with a cup of tea, and more than 1,000 shop windows displayed British goods.

During the opening ceremony, speeches were given in front of a large, house-like cube decorated with union-jacks in the Piazza Duomo, by both the Mayor of Milan and the Lord Mayor of London, before a cloud of red, white and blue balloons were released.

The Churchill Crown

Sir Winston Churchill has become the latest recipient of a commemorative crown coin. On one side of the coin will be the uncrowned effigy of the Queen, on the other, a portrait of Sir Winston, with the word *'Churchill'*. Although technically legal tender, the coins will not be in general circulation, but orders have already exceeded seven million, far eclipsing the Queen's coronation crown record of 5.5 million. Surprisingly, overseas orders have contributed more than expected, with at least three million coming from the US.

The crown coin has enjoyed a varied tenure in British currency, with frequent changes in value, manufacturing and metal content since its first iteration in 1544. The first crown, commissioned by Henry VIII, was made from 22 carat gold, with a value of five shillings. It was embossed with the King's face and was commonly referred to as *'the crown of the Double Rose',* an ode to his father's settling of the Wars of the Roses. Edward IV oversaw the second Crown coin, this time made from silver. This was the first British coin to feature a date stamp, in Arabic numerals, and set a precedent for silver coinage as currency. Over the next two centuries, a number of other iterations were published, each following the stylistic pattern set by Henry VIII. Queen Victoria saw four different crown designs for her coin: a youthful portrait with a bare head in 1839; a *'gothic'* design with a crown and embroidered dress in 1847; a golden jubilee design in 1887, and a *'widowed'* coin in 1893. Queen Victoria's successor, Edward VII's 1902 coronation crown became the last coin to be used in general circulation. Since then, the crown coins have been used for commemorative purposes, with their monetary value based on what the 'going rate' is.

Oct 15th – 21st 1965

IN THE NEWS

Friday 15 — **"Royal Opening"** The Queen inaugurated the North of Scotland Hydro-Electric Board's £12 million pumped storage scheme at Loch Awe, despite heavy rain and harsh winds. The ceremony took place in the machine hall, accessed through a three-quarters of a mile long tunnel inside a mountain.

Saturday 16 — **"Deep Water Berths"** The Mersey Docks and Harbour Board announced plans for the construction of 14 new deep-water berths just north of Liverpool. The development, costing £36 million, should be available for use by 1971.

Sunday 17 — **"Thames Barrage"** A barrage spanning 28 miles across the mouth of the Thames, between Clacton and Margate, was suggested by a group at the Royal Institution of Chartered Surveyors. The plans would dam off the London region from tidal surges.

Monday 18 — **"Submariners on the Rise"** The submarine branch of the Royal Navy is to be increased from 3,500 to 4,500 personnel, to crew the new Polaris nuclear submarines.

Tuesday 19 — **"The Catacombs Opened"** The Catacombs Coffee Club, set up by a group of Christian workers to combat the spread of drugs amongst youths in Manchester, was opened by the Bishop of Hulme.

Wednesday 20 — **"No Royal Photographs"** Press photographers refused to take pictures of the Queen and Duke of Edinburgh as they arrived by train into Euston Station in protest against not being allowed within 70 metres of Her Majesty disembarking.

Thursday 21 — **"Comet-Cam"** Photographers were told to be on high alert just before dawn to see the Ikeya-Seki comet pass over Britain. The object was the most vivid since the 1910 return of Halley's Comet, 40 times brighter than Venus.

HERE IN BRITAIN

"Gift to the Nation"

The Brecon Beacons and surrounding moorland area has been gifted to the National Trust by the Eagle Star Insurance Company. 7,700 acres of land were presented *'to the nation'* by the company's chairman, aptly named, Sir Brian Mountain, an avid mountaineer.

Eagle Star acquired the land as part of a £750,000 purchase of the Tredegar Estate in 1957. The transaction included *Pen-y-fan* mountain which, at a height of 2,907 ft, is the tallest in southern Wales and a commemorative cairn is to be erected in honour of the gift, at the summit of the mountain.

AROUND THE WORLD

"Vietnam Conscription"

The US Defence Department asked for the conscription of over 45,000 men, 10,000 more than the previous draft, and the largest since the Korean War over a decade ago. The conscripts will join the already 150,000 troop-strong US presence in Vietnam in their ongoing struggle against the communist Vietcong.

The announcement comes amidst rife protests against continued involvement, especially in student dense areas, and it is thought that this new draft will spark harsher criticism of the war. The army is set to receive 40,000 troops, with the Marines taking the other 5,000.

Trafalgar Day

Thursday 21st October
Trafalgar Day Lunch
Join us to commemorate Nelson's famous victory

Trafalgar Day is an annual celebration observed on October 21, commemorating the Royal Navy's victory over the French and Spanish at the Battle of Trafalgar in 1805. France was the dominant military force led by Napoleon, a great soldier. However, the Royal Navy ruled the seas and, in this battle, Nelson captured 18 French ships, forcing Admiral Villeneuve to surrender.

However, the Battle of Trafalgar is perhaps remembered most for the death of Admiral Horatio Nelson aboard HMS Victory. His body was placed in a cask of brandy mixed with camphor and myrrh, which was then lashed to the Victory's mainmast and placed under guard. At Gibraltar the body was transferred to a lead-lined coffin filled with spirits of wine. Arriving eventually at the Nore on the Thames, Nelson's body was placed inside a lead coffin which was encased in a wooden one made from the mast of his ship 'L'Orient' which had been salvaged after his greatest victory, the Battle of the Nile. After a four-hour service at St. Paul's Cathedral, he was finally interred within the crypt, in a black marble sarcophagus originally carved for Cardinal Wolsey.

Nelson's skill and bravery was such that he was claimed a national hero, with many monuments erected throughout Britain in the years following his death. On Trafalgar Day, his monuments are decorated with flags, banners or laurel swags, and wreath laying ceremonies are held during the day in his honour when the famous Trafalgar flag signal "England expects that every man will do his duty" is flown from Nelson's Column in London and on Carleton Hill, Edinburgh. In the evening, at specially held commemorative Trafalgar Night dinners, a speech is made which always ends with a toast to "The Immortal Memory of Lord Nelson, and those who fell with him".

Oct 22nd – 28th 1965

IN THE NEWS

Friday 22 — **"Chaos on the Motorway"** More than 100 vehicles were damaged in accidents along the M4, seven of which were abandoned on the hard shoulder. Visibility on the motorway was barely five yards, causing stationary traffic and two-mile-queues.

Saturday 23 — **"HMS Churchill"** In memory of the late wartime Prime Minister, Britain's fourth nuclear-powered submarine has been ordered, named *HMS Churchill*. The announcement was made at a Trafalgar Night dinner in Lee-on-Solent.

Sunday 24 — **"United Nations Day"** As 700 tourists from the Soviet Union disembarked the *Alexander Pushkin* liner at Tilbury, British tourists took their place, eager to see the conditions of the Soviet lifestyle. Over 2,000 Britons had a look around the Russian ship.

Monday 25 — **"Jubilant Africans Greet Mr Wilson"** In response to those African countries asking that the UK use force to prevent Rhodesia from declaring unilateral independence, the Prime Minister travelled to Salisbury for talks to *'avert what he was certain would be a tragedy'.*

Tuesday 26 — **"Royal Union Card"** Princess Margaret become an honorary member of the *National Society of Operative Printers and Assistants,* making her eligible to open the new Birmingham Post and Mail building.

Wednesday 27 — **"Deaths from Crash"** Thirty-six people onboard a British European Airways Vanguard aircraft from Edinburgh to London Airport died when the aircraft ran into difficulties in foggy conditions. This was London airport's first passenger crash in ten years.

Thursday 28 — **"Big Brass in the City"** During filming for *The Big Brass,* the Ministry of Aviation permitted a jet aircraft, nicknamed *'Grassi',* to fly as low as 1,000ft over the rooftops of the city of London. Two runs were completed at reduced power.

HERE IN BRITAIN

"London Motor Show"

Orders flooded in as the London Motor Show got underway. British car manufacturers saw record sales, with Aston Martin taking more than £1.5 million worth of orders for their new DB6. Yet, the success in sales was marred by some extensive damage.

Although broken switches, scratched bodywork and cracked windows happen to show cars, salesmen reported more extreme vandalism to many exhibits. Rolls-Royce witnessed people stealing cigarette lighters, someone ripping away a heavy leather padded arm rest, and even smashing a door lock.

AROUND THE WORLD

"Just the Same as Us"

The correspondence columns of Chinese provincial newspapers offer unrivalled insight into life under the communist regime, proving life 5,000 miles away is not so different to the trials and tribulations of Londoners.

A recent edition of a Canton evening newspaper highlighted the opinions of bus passengers in China: *'the bus is about to move ... several passengers run behind and try to board it. But the door is slammed shut.'* This analysis by a conductor was followed by the conclusion that drivers should take more care and appreciation for passengers.

NOBEL PRIZES

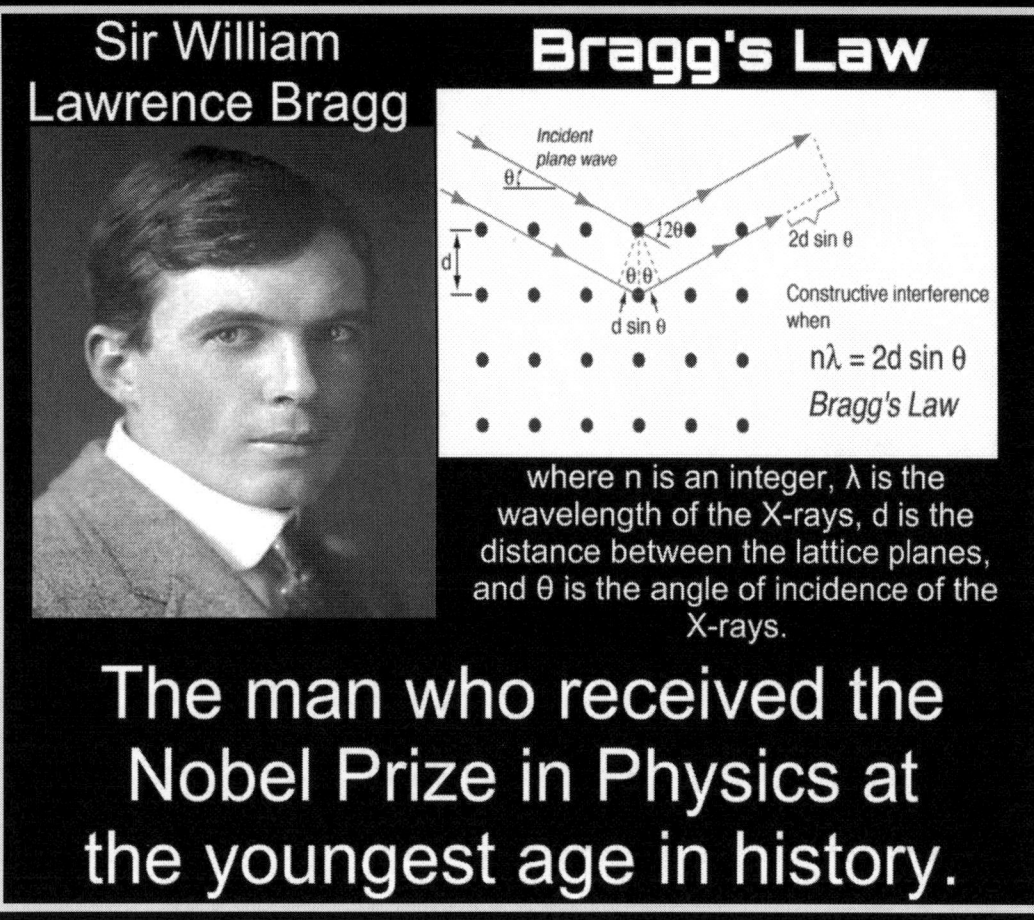

Sir William Lawrence Bragg

Bragg's Law

Constructive interference when
$$n\lambda = 2d \sin \theta$$
Bragg's Law

where n is an integer, λ is the wavelength of the X-rays, d is the distance between the lattice planes, and θ is the angle of incidence of the X-rays.

The man who received the Nobel Prize in Physics at the youngest age in history.

Former British winners of a Nobel Prize were gathered at the Royal British Institute for the fiftieth anniversary of the award, presented this year to Sir Lawrence Bragg, Director of the institution, for his work on X-Ray crystallography. Of the 28 living British recipients, 22 attended the occasion, and the Swedish Ambassador presented the award.

Between 1901 and 1965, 320 Nobel prizes have been awarded to 1,000 people and organisations, in what has become one of the most prestigious scientific recognition awards on the planet. The international event is administered by the Swedish-based Nobel Foundation, named after scientist, engineer and businessman, Alfred Nobel. Nobel is possibly best known for inventing dynamite in 1867, but also made countless other contributions to science, culminating in 335 patents in his name prior to his death in 1896. Nobel was fluent in six languages by age 20, filed his first patent aged 24, and was the owner of a major weapon and armaments business for most of his life. In his will, Nobel donated his substantial fortune to fund the *Nobel Prizes,* to be bestowed upon those who *'conferred the greatest benefit to mankind.'* It was decided that the Royal Swedish Academy of Sciences, of whom Nobel was a member, would be responsible for choosing the Nobel Laureates in both physics and chemistry. Each prize consists of a green-gold medal, made from 24 carat gold, a personal diploma and a cash prize exceeding $1 million. The prize is awarded to individuals from five different fields every year: physics, chemistry, medicine, literature and peace.

It is thought that, in 1888, Nobel was profoundly sad after reading his own obituary entitled *'The Merchant of Death is Dead'*, prompting him to create the award. This theory has not been verified and may well be a myth.

Oct 29th - Nov 4th 1965

IN THE NEWS

Friday 29 — **"Cathedral Vandalism"** Kent police are investigating the work of *'thoughtless thugs'* who vandalised Canterbury Cathedral during holy communion. The word 'PEACE' was painted in red across the front of both the Nave and High Altars.

Saturday 30 — **"No Appeal from the PM"** Harold Wilson flew back from Rhodesia leaving a *'small British foot'* in the door between an independence grab and a settlement of the crisis, despite the decision not to allow him to make a TV broadcast direct to the Rhodesian people.

Sunday 31 — **"Schooner Toppled"** The 300-ton top-sail schooner, Sir Winston Churchill, toppled off her slipway at Hessle Shipyard in Hull ahead of the official launch next week. Seven men were taken to hospital for their injuries.

Monday Nov 1 — **"Cooling Coming Down"** The 350ft tall cooling towers set to be fitted to Europe's biggest power station in Yorkshire were blown down by wind during construction. Most of the site's 2,500 workers were on their breaks, and no one was hurt.

Tuesday 2 — **"Proxy Vote Plan"** MPs unable to attend sittings of the House of Commons, due to illness or being away on business, may soon be able to vote remotely. The change will mean that the government, with a majority of three, has a far greater chance of survival.

Wednesday 3 — **"Leather Girls"** 16 *'leather girls'*, members of the British Leatherwear Fashion Expert Group, returned from their excursion to New York Harbour, where they had showcased British products aboard the liner 'Queen Elizabeth'.

Thursday 4 — **"Chemical Thieves"** Enough strychnine nitrate to wipe out the population of a large city was stolen from London Airport. The 30lbs box is enough to *'wipe out 500,000 people'* according to a pharmacist.

HERE IN BRITAIN

"Thames Wales"

30 pilot whales, some over 20ft in length, could be seen in the River Thames just off Northfleet. People rushed to the riverbanks, or went out in small boats to view the animals at close range; a representative of Billy Smart's Circus was amongst them, hoping to catch one of the whales – but in a boat that was far too small. Police prevented any capture attempts, as all Thames inhabitants are the property of the Crown. The whales' presence has been attributed to the river cleanup project of recent years.

AROUND THE WORLD

"Land Speed Record"

Craig Breedlove, driving his jet-powered car *Spirit of America,* achieved a new land speed record of 555.127 miles an hour, breaking the previous record held by Art Arfons, by over 19 mph. The attempt took two runs along the Utah salt flats, and it is thought that Arfons will return to challenge the record.

Breedlove's *'jet car'* uses a parachute braking system. According to reports, Breedlove will next be *'aiming for 600'* on his return to the flats, with only the first of his three-part afterburner firing correctly.

Going A-Guising

Scottish Children 'Guising'

The origins of Halloween can be traced back to the ancient Celtic festival of Samhain. The year was divided according to the growing seasons, and Samhain marked the end of summer and the harvest, and the beginning of the dark, cold winter. Among Celtic-speaking peoples, All Hallows Eve was seen as a liminal or 'thin' time, when the spirits or fairies and the souls of the dead came into our world to be appeased with offerings of food and drink. The festival symbolised the boundary between the world of the living and the world of the dead and large bonfires were lit in each village to ward off any spirits who were evil. All house fires were put out and new fires lit from these great bonfires.

This was the time when Scottish children would dress up and pretend to be malicious spirits as they went 'guising' around the local streets, walking from house to house. It was believed that, by disguising themselves, they would blend in with any wandering spirits and remain safe from harm. In true Scottish tradition, scary faces were carved into neeps (turnips) to create lanterns that would scare off ghouls wandering in the witching hours. They would put on a small performance at each house - usually singing a song or reciting a joke or a funny poem. After performing tricks or songs, guisers were given food or gifts as a reward for the performance. One food however, that should be shunned at Hallowe'en, is the humble sausage roll. Due to pork's loose connection with witchcraft, pork bones being commonly used in spells, apples and sweets are probably a safer bet. Because you never quite know who you could have standing on your doorstep, on a cold dark evening at the end of October…..

Nov 5ᵀᴴ - 11ᵀᴴ 1965

IN THE NEWS

Friday 5 — **"State of Emergency"** Rhodesian Prime Minister Ian Smith has officially imposed a State of Emergency, turning the country into a complete police state. A UK cabinet meeting has been called in case the situation escalates into an independence grab.

Saturday 6 — **"Under Attack"** British warships have been warned about a new *'menace from above'*, pedestrians throwing coins and stones from the new Forth Road Bridge. Authorities have threatened sanctions to all those caught throwing projectiles.

Sunday 7 — **"The Bremer Run"** The first four-wheeled car built in Britain, the 1894 single-cylinder *Bremer,* became the oldest car to complete the RAC's London to Brighton race, finishing the 54-mile course in seven hours and 55 minutes. A total of 199 cars made it to Brighton in time to qualify, including the only surviving competitor of the first race in 1894.

Monday 8 — **"Abolition of Murder"** The Royal Assent was given to the Murder Bill, officially ending capital punishment for murder in England, Scotland and Wales.

Tuesday 9 — **"Weather Radar"** New radar controls are being implemented to regulate the speed of cars on the M6 during foggy conditions. The initiative also includes an increase in the number of motorway patrol cars.

Wednesday 10 — **"Rig Demand"** Due to a sudden expansion in offshore oil and natural gas drilling, the availability of drilling rigs is becoming scarcer. Largely attributed to a shortage in skilled labour, a rig costs £3 million to produce, and a further £6,000 per day to operate.

Thursday 11 — **"Unilateral Declaration of Independence"** The Government wasted no time in retaliating to Rhodesia's Unilateral Declaration of Independence, swiftly imposing trade restrictions on sugar and tobacco, 70% of the country's exports to Britain.

HERE IN BRITAIN

"Abolition of the Death Penalty"

The Royal Assent was given to the Murder (Abolition of the Death Penalty) Bill, the culmination of a century's worth of campaigning by activists.

The reform came in staccato form: in 1868, public executions stopped; 1908, the death sentence on children under 16 was abolished; 1921, the Howard League for Penal Reform was established; 1925, the National Council for the Abolition of the Death Penalty was founded; and 1957, the Homicide Act made way for the final abolition of capital punishment.

AROUND THE WORLD

"Sotheby's Sale Rooms"

The usual Friday furniture sale at Sotheby's this week included an astonishing piece that no collector dared to value beforehand; an American flag with 15 pointed stars and eight white and seven blue stripes, dating it as early as 1794.

The flag hails from a time just after Kentucky and Vermont had been admitted to the Union, and was submitted by a descendent of the owner, who had been presented with the flag by the first Governor of Maryland in 1797. The flag was sold at auction to the President of Calvert Distillers for £5,400.

ROYAL VARIETY PERFORMANCE

Her Majesty the Queen was dressed in a full-length evening dress, fur stole and glittering tiara for 'Theatreland's biggest night of the year', the Royal Variety Performance. All the top names in show business descended on the London Palladium, including comedian Spike Milligan, who made the Duke of Edinburgh roar with laughter during his sketch about Prince Charles' planned stay at a school in Australia.

This prestigious event dates back to 1912, when King George V and his wife, Queen Mary, attended a 'Royal Command' performance at the Palace Theatre in Cambridge. The event, furnished with over 3 million roses, was in aid of the Variety Artistes' Benevolent Fund's scheme to build an extension to its care home for elderly entertainers. To this day, the event still ranks as one of the most successful in the performance's history, with all the great names of British entertainment in attendance: all that is, except Marie Lloyd, arguably one of the biggest musicians of those early days. She refused to attend on the grounds that her performance was 'too risqué' for Royal entertainment, sparking one of the biggest controversies in the event's history. There was just one moment in the inaugural performance that caused unease: male impersonator Vesta Tilley displeased Queen Mary, who, disapproving of the notion that a woman should come on stage dressed in trousers like a man, covered her face with her programme. Nevertheless, joviality was soon restored by her successor, the great comic Harry Tate.

The second iteration of the event saw the change of name to 'the Royal Variety Performance', in order to 'reflect all areas of show business popular amongst the masses of the time.' The change came at the request of the Royal Family, who wanted the event to be perceived not as one of their own entertainment preferences, but instead of the nations'.

Nov 12th – 18th 1965

IN THE NEWS

Friday 12 — **"Floodlit Crashes"** Experiments with floodlights are to be conducted by the Police at the scenes of major accidents, especially along the M4 motorway. A Land Rover containing floodlights will be on constant patrol and attend the scenes of serious accidents.

Saturday 13 — **"***** BBC"** The BBC has apologised for the use of a *'four letter expletive'* during a performance on BBC 3 by Kenneth Tynan, the Drama Critic. Hundreds of viewers complained when Mr Tynan swore during an unscripted discussion of his views.

Sunday 14 — **"Remembrance Sunday"** The Queen and Duke of Edinburgh joined veterans from both World Wars for the annual Remembrance Service at the Cenotaph in Whitehall.

Monday 15 — **"Winter Blackout"** Severe weather caused blackouts and power-outages across the country. In London an hour of reduced electrical power caused a complete shut off in many suburbs, and people in the West Midlands were urged to switch off their household appliances *'at once'* to conserve energy.

Tuesday 16 — **"Health Boards"** The British Medical Association Council concluded that Wales is most suitable to begin experiments into *'health boards.'* The scheme would link the three branches of the NHS more efficiently- hospitals, welfare services, and GP services.

Wednesday 17 — **"Concord Engine"** The first test of the Bristol Siddeley-Snecma Olympus 593B jet engine was completed ahead of schedule. The engine is set to power the Anglo-French *Concord* supersonic airliner.

Thursday 18 — **"Baker's Strike"** Over a million homes will be unable to purchase bread until next Monday due to a bakery workers strike. The strike comes following employers' refusal to meet workers' demands for a £15 basic wage and 40-hour week.

HERE IN BRITAIN

"WANTED: Twelfth Juror"

At the start of a trial at Guildford, a defence barrister objected to a juror at the swearing-in ceremony. The deputy Recorder asked a police inspector to search for a twelfth man. The procedure evokes an old Act permitting someone to *'go into the street and ask anybody passing by to sit on the jury.'*

So, for thirty minutes the inspector searched for a householder over 21, under 60, with a house of more than 15 windows, and living in the borough area. After two failed attempts, a suitable replacement was finally found and the trial got underway.

AROUND THE WORLD

"Land Speed Records"

Donald Campbell's world land speed record for a vehicle driven through their wheels was beaten by 6mph. The Summer brothers from Ontario, California, reached 409.277mph along the Utah Salt Flats in their 32-foot-long needle shaped car, known as *Goldenrod*.

The record comes in the same week that fellow American Craig Breedlove, set the record for a jet-propelled car in the same location, with a speed of 600.601mph. Breedlove became the first man to *'beat the 600'*, and broke his own record of 576mph that he set just two weeks prior.

THE LORD MAYOR'S SHOW

Fruit was the theme of this year's Lord Mayor's Show, in honour of Sir Lionel Denny, the incoming London City Mayor. Denny, a produce importer, led the procession to the law courts, where he was sworn in with a traditional ceremony. Spitalfields market porters accompanied Sir Lionel with handbarrows loaded with fruit, alongside 18 colourful floats filled with students distributing produce to children. Pop group, the *Apple-Jacks,* provided musical entertainment, and floats from countries all across the world showcased more traditional elements of British, Commonwealth and international cultures.

The Lord Mayor's Show is the oldest running civic procession in the world, with shows dating back to the 13th Century. Originally a festival in celebration of London's independence, the Show has since evolved into a demonstration of quintessential British pomp and circumstance. A nervous King John in the 13th Century, during a time of monarchical and political Medieval turmoil, permitted the appointment of a London Mayor, but in turn required he make the journey to Westminster to be sworn in by the King's own Divine Right. From this event blossomed 800 years of tradition, with the pageant occurring every year on the Feast of St Simon and St Jude, 28th October, until 1751. The adoption of the Gregorian Calendar, removing a large chunk of September, forced the ceremony to be brought back to the 9th November to ensure the correct Mayoral term length. It has remained on this day for the past 200 years.

It was only in the 16th Century that the procession became a show of entertainment for Londoners, when the then Lord Mayor decided to employ the use of 15,000 locals, dressed in coats of white silk; a display of such eccentricity that the authorities were on high alert for fears of revolt. .

Nov 19th - 25th 1965

IN THE NEWS

Friday 19 — **"Sea Cow Tragedy"** Three men died, and 13 others were injured when the 'Sea Cow' drilling barge they were on was shattered by an explosion, sinking into 30ft of water when drilling into the rocky riverbed off Tees dock in Middlesborough to provide a deep water for the quay of the new Shell oil refinery.

Saturday 20 — **"Explosive Water"** A warning was given to all shipping using the Tees, including fishermen and sailing clubs. They have been warned of unexploded gelignite floating loose on the water, part of the load from the Sea Cow explosion yesterday.

Sunday 21 — **"The Starlings Returned"** Psychological warfare is the latest tactic of Glasgow Council in their ongoing war with starlings. They are using compressed air hoses and searchlights to scare the birds from their perches. But, as one boy observed, *'they're all coming back.'*

Monday 22 — **"Snow Chaos"** Icy conditions caused havoc on motorways in many areas in northern Britain. The weather, spreading southwards from Scotland, forced 17 miles of the M1 to close for two hours following multiple crashes.

Tuesday 23 — **"Enough Shilling's for the Meter"** The Royal Mint confirmed that there are over one million shillings in circulation across Britain, ample amounts to satisfy gas and electricity metres for the winter months.

Wednesday 24 — **"Temporary Speed Limit"** An experimental 70mph speed limit will be imposed on over 100,000 miles of currently unrestricted roads, including motorways. The Minister of Transport blamed the *'irresponsibility of a minority of drivers'*.

Thursday 25 — **"Mini Cooper Success"** For the first time, a Mini-Cooper S, driven by Finn, Rauno Aaltonen, won the 2,350-mile International Rally of Great Britain.

HERE IN BRITAIN

"Sea-Bound Pigeon"

Beatrice is a pigeon with an insatiable urge for sailing the seas. After landing on the Norwegian freighter *Bruno* last June, she has sailed 40,000 miles around the Atlantic as the ship's pet. Upon arrival in London, the crew, thinking it wasn't fair to subject a bird to life at sea, took her via Underground to Trafalgar Square, where she was released. Early retirement clearly didn't fly with Beatrice, who was found waiting on deck for the crew's return. Since, she has travelled 900 miles through the Amazon, with the ship's radio officer documenting her progress.

AROUND THE WORLD

"A Dark Place of Crime"

Britain has been described by the official Chinese news agency as a *'dark place of crime, hooliganism and debauchery'* where *'citizens fear for their lives because of road accidents and gangs'*. In the only news outlet that transmits foreign news to the Chinese people, British crime statistics were used to demonstrate the *'decay of the capitalist system'*. *'Filthy films, novels, television shows, crazy music and the Twist, alcoholism and gambling, all sow the seeds of crime'* and London is the *'holy land'* of criminals with *'obscene magazines and booklets'* imported from the USA.

MISS WORLD

Britain retained the Miss World Title it won last year, with Miss Lesley Langley, a 21-year-old blonde from Weymouth, Dorset clinching the 1965 title. This year's event was held at the Lyceum Ballroom in London, where Langley won the full prize pot of £2,500 ahead of second place, Miss USA, and third place, Miss Ireland. *'The first thing I'm going to do with the money is to find a nice flat'* said Miss Langley, who seemed shocked to come away with victory.

The 1965 contest wasn't without its controversy; earlier in the evening, press photographers staged a mass walk out after a shouting match with the organisational director, Eric Morley. Morley told the photographers to sit down during the first parade to make way for the BBC, who had paid £3,000 for television rights: *'gentlemen, would you please sit down. We all know only the winner's picture will appear in the papers in the morning, there is no point taking pictures of the others. Do not get in the way of the BBC.'* Morley later apologised to the photographers, who eventually came back.

Miss World is the longest running international beauty pageant, having first been held in 1951. British television presenter Eric Morley organised a bikini contest as part of the Festival of Britain, which many people, including the British press, chose to dub as *Miss World*. The event drew widespread interest from fans and critics alike, with many seeing the bikini, a relatively new garment at the time, as unbecoming of a woman. The event was originally meant to be a 'one off', but its popularity meant that Morley brought it back in subsequent years, earning himself the nickname *Mr World*. By 1959, the BBC had begun broadcasting the event, and it soon became one of the most watched programmes of the 1960s.

Nov 26th – Dec 2nd 1965

IN THE NEWS

Friday 26 — **"Churchill Crowns"** Delays in fulfilling orders for 12 million of the 5 shilling Churchill Crown coins means that coin dealers are reselling them at a premium, for 7s 6d. The Royal Mint has assured customers that no special treatment is being given to collectors.

Saturday 27 — **"Seeing the Lights"** The thousands of people who drove to see the Christmas lights in London's West End caused major congestion along Oxford Street and Regent Street.

Sunday 28 — **"The Worst for 20 Years"** Road conditions in the north of England and Scotland have been described as *'the worst in November for 20 years'* as fresh snow up to eight inches fell in Aberdeenshire.

Monday 29 — **"Clean-Up-TV"** The Clean-Up-TV Campaign, *'that scourge of decadence, dirt, and disbelief on the small screen'* has changed to the National Viewers' and Listeners' Association. The organisation will usurp the old movement, and in doing so, widen its objectives.

Tuesday 30 — **"More Turkeys"** Six million turkeys, over 500,000 more than last year, will be available for this year's Christmas Market, claims the chairman of the British Turkey Foundation. One-in-three households will be able to purchase a bird for their Christmas dinner.

Wed Dec 1 — **"The Ford GT"** The fastest Ford ever sold to the public, the road version of the Ford GT Le Mans challenger, went on sale in Britain. Capable of 150mph, the car costs more than £6,500 and on its first day, dealers received 30 orders.

Thursday 2 — **"Non-Stop-Pop"** In the Government's ongoing review of broadcasting, it was decided that it would be too difficult to legislate Pirate radio stations off air. Also, it could be political suicide, as a large number of young voters enjoy the radio's *'non-stop-pop'*.

HERE IN BRITAIN

"Medieval Extension"

Craftsmen skilled in using medieval tools and traditional crafting methods have been employed for the £175,000 renovation and extension of the medieval Swan Hotel in Lavenham, Suffolk. The extensions include the old Wool Hall and the adjacent buildings, and the work was carried out to match, as closely as possible, the earlier fabrics used, to an unusually successful degree. The architect, a retired Trust House employee, hopes that the hotel will stand for *'another 500 years'* because of the modern improvements to the building's structural integrity. Trust House Hotels have owned the Swan since 1933.

AROUND THE WORLD

"Medical Assistance"

Jamaican trained nurses who are now working in Britain are being begged to return to their homeland to help ease the severe staff shortage in the country. Following an official plea from the Jamaican Government, the High Commissioner in London sent a letter to all regional hospitals in the country, drawing attention to their difficulties, and lobbying them to display it on noticeboards. Although there are between 2,000 and 3,000 qualified Jamaican nurses in Britain, the Jamaican Government was very quick to assure Britain that they only wanted as many as the NHS could spare.

Stir Up Sunday

'Stir-up Sunday' is a centuries old tradition, where on the last Sunday before Advent, housewives start 'stirring up' their Christmas puddings. It is a family affair, and even children are allowed to help weigh out and mix all the ingredients ready for steaming the pudding. Everyone is expected to take a turn to stir the pudding mix, for each person can make a special wish for the year ahead. Traditionally, the pudding should be stirred from east to west, in honour of the Wise Men who travelled from the East to visit the baby Jesus.

Rich Christmas puddings and fruit cakes benefit from being made this much in advance because it allows the flavours to intensify, and the colour deepen over time. Puddings can be re-steamed each week and many people will also 'feed' their cakes by pricking the base and pouring an eggcup full of brandy or rum over it, before wrapping it up again carefully to preserve the moisture. By Christmas, a good cake or pudding will be 'black and rotten' – very rich indeed!

The Christmas pudding originated in the 14th-century as a sort of porridge, originally known as 'frumenty', which bore little resemblance to the pudding we know today but, in the 17th century, changes to the recipe were made. It was thickened with eggs, breadcrumbs, dried fruit and beer or spirits were added – and it came to resemble something a bit more like a sweet pudding. Nowadays, the ingredients include raisins, currants, suet, brown sugar, breadcrumbs, carrot, mixed peel, flour, mixed spices, eggs, milk and brandy, which are all essential for keeping qualities. Puddings were traditionally boiled in a 'pudding cloth', although today are usually steamed in a basin, then brought to the table with a sprig of holly, doused in brandy and set alight.

Dec 3rd – Dec 9th 1965

IN THE NEWS

Friday 3 — **"Fairer to the Motorist"** Motorists who defy speed limits in Marlow, Buckinghamshire, are being fined 10s (50p) for each mile in excess of the speed limit. This means that, to be awarded the maximum fine of £50, you would need to travel 130mph in a 30 zone.

Saturday 4 — **"Shining a Light on Car Safety"** Of the 1,385 vehicles that passed through AA car light test stations, just 173 were found to have all their lights in order. This confirms the findings of the AA's national survey last year.

Sunday 5 — **"Radioactive"** Radioactive liquid will be discharged into the Firth of Forth from the Royal Navy's nuclear submarine maintenance dock, Rosyth Dockyard. The river authorities have assured that there will be no danger.

Monday 6 — **"Refit for the Queen Elizabeth"** The 83,000-ton liner, The Queen Elizabeth, returned to her birthplace for a one million-pound, four month, refit at Greenock dry dock.

Tuesday 7 — **"Press Button Control"** Telephone buttons with ten press-buttons instead of finger-holes, will be tried out over the next three months among 300 subscribers on the Langham exchange in London. The buttons are arranged in two rows of five numbers, but later versions are expected to have three rows of three, with the zero underneath.

Wednesday 8 — **"Race Relations Act"** The Race Relations Act of 1965 was given royal assent; this was the first act in the UK to address racial discrimination.

Thursday 9 — **"Reactivation of Capenhurst"** The 'modernisation' and 'reactivation' of the Capenhurst, Cheshire, plant of atomic energy enrichment, is to begin immediately. The scheme, announced by the Minister of Technology, is set to cost £13.5 million.

HERE IN BRITAIN

"The Day They Deserted Work"

On Tuesday the 7th December, streets in the centre of Glasgow between 1:30pm and 3:15pm were completely female dominated, because so many men were watching the football match between Scotland and Italy.
Scotland needed to beat Italy away in Naples to qualify for the World Cup; alas, the final score was 3-0 to Italy. The mass absenteeism in the city forced a number of factories and workshops to close, despite threats of punishment from company officials. Rolls Royce kept their workers happy by offering updated bulletins every 15 minutes.

AROUND THE WORLD

"Anti Locust Campaign"

The World Meteorological Association has acknowledged its role in the ongoing anti-locust campaign. Swarms of the *'flying machine'* insects have ravaged the continent in recent weeks, with the swarms able to exist for weeks on end, covering hundreds of miles in distance. In the largest recorded invasion in East Africa.

100 million insects, weighing over 200 million tons, covered an area of 800 square miles. The insects are capable of eating their own weight in vegetation daily. It is hoped that meteorological reports will help facilitate dispersing the swarms.

CHRISTMAS SHOPPING

Since the 8,000 Christmas lights in London were switched on last week, thousands of shoppers have descended on Selfridges to get ahead on their Christmas shopping. Selfridges boasted new and improved shopping experiences and facilities this year, with a number of items making their debut on the Christmas shelves: automatic playing card shufflers and a *'charming little'* filigree box designed to hold after eight chocolates, for just 4 guineas, are just some of the quirky stocking-fillers available. One of the perks of the nearby Regent Street shopping hub is the pleasure of parking safely, for an hour a day, at Lex car park. From there, a motorist can ask for their parcels to be brought out directly to the car, and even receive a car wash while they shop.

Some of the most gifts included the American-made Thermo-Spoon, capable of recording cooking temperatures up to 450 degrees Fahrenheit and a golden goose container for saccharine for the tea tray at just one guinea, and in Dickens & Jones, there was a Scandinavian-made seat for a toddler shaped like a turtle for 3 guineas and a scrub-a-tub bath cleaner at 8s 11d.

Fun to open Grocery Boxes returned to shelves, weighted down with delicious items from Selfridges' food halls, and immediately became a family favourite. Costing between 25s and 20 guineas, the hampers can be delivered to anywhere in Britain for free. New this year are dietetic slimming boxes, containing a number of salt-free and low-calorie foods for just £4. For two weeks already, the bells of the new clock outside Fortnum and Mason in Piccadilly have been playing Christmas carols at each hour between 8am and 11pm, enticing shoppers to embrace the festive spirit.

Dec 10th – 16th 1965

IN THE NEWS

Friday 10 — **"Sheer Damn Laziness"** The increase of imports of manufactured goods to Britain is due to the *'Sheer damn laziness'* of British industry letting other countries get ahead, according to the Prime Minister who also called for a *'full day's work for a full day's pay'*.

Saturday 11 — **"Gale Chaos"** Extreme winds and floods wreaked havoc in parts of London as the River Thames burst its banks in Southend and Essex. Police were on high alert to warn pedestrians and respond to reports.

Sunday 12 — **"Stolen Goods On Shop Shelves"** Two police raids on shops in London retrieved another haul of jewellery, gold, silver, furs and relics, bringing the total value of goods confiscated in the capital this year, to over £1 million.

Monday 13 — **"Arms for Saudi"** Britain has beaten the US in securing arms contracts with Saudi Arabia estimated to be worth at least £107 million; Saudi Arabia placed orders for a comprehensive air defence system.

Tuesday 14 — **"Equal Validity"** The Government accepted the recommendation of the Hughes Parry committee for equal validity of the Welsh and English languages in Wales. The Secretary of State affirmed that it would not impair the rights of those who speak English.

Wednesday 15 — **"Gemini 6 Meets 7"** The United States broke another milestone in the space race, becoming the first to orchestrate the rendezvous of man in space, when the *Gemini 6* spacecraft, met up with its companion, *Gemini 7*.

Thursday 16 — **"Grade-Rive"** Britain's new cinema circuit, *Grade-Rive*, is to begin showing both British and foreign high-quality films in a number of small, luxurious cinemas throughout Britain, in cities where the company feels they can get the largest audiences.

HERE IN BRITAIN

"Goldie the Eagle"

Goldie the Eagle escaped from London Zoo for the second time this year, after flying out the door whilst his keeper was leaving. Goldie remained at large in Regent's Park throughout the night, not falling for the lures of food put out by the zoo handlers.

The great bird first escaped in February, remaining at large for 12 days in the park amidst large crowds and publicity. Goldie gobbled up a Muscovy duck, was chased by dogs, and narrowly missed catching a snow goose; eventually he was caught by a rabbit food lure.

AROUND THE WORLD

"Troops In Trees"

American helicopters in Vietnam are set to land US troops in treetops, following the invention of wire-mesh landing platforms. The devices, that can be laid out across the tops in less than 10 minutes, are 200ft long and 50ft wide.

At present helicopters are forced to land in cleared areas, indicating plans of attack to the enemy but once the 1st Airborne Cavalry Division are successfully trained in mounting the portable platforms onto the jungle canopy, this innovation is set to help combat the insurgent Vietcong.

The Trafalgar Tree

Norway's annual gift of a Christmas tree is in pride of place at Trafalgar Square. The 63-foot, four ton, tree, is one of the most impressive yet, and thousands of people flocked to London on the 10th of December to watch the Norwegian Ambassador ceremoniously switch the tree lights on. London's Regent Street and Oxford Street Christmas illuminations were switched on last week.

The first tree was sent from Oslo in 1947 as a token of gratitude to the British people for their help during the second world war when Great Britain was Norway's closest ally. London was where the Norwegian King Haakon VII and his government fled as their country was occupied, and it was from here that much of Norway's resistance movement was organised. Both the BBC and its Norwegian counterpart NRK would broadcast in Norwegian from London, something that was both an important source of information and a boost of morale for those who remained in Norway, where people would listen in secret to their forbidden radios. The idea to send a pine to Britain was first conceived by the Norwegian naval commando, Mons Urangsvå, who sent a tree from the island of Hisøy which had been cut down during a raid to London in 1942 as a gift to King Haakon and King George V decided that it should be installed in Trafalgar Square where it stood *'evergreen with defiant hope'*.

The trees come from the snow-covered forest area surrounding Oslo, known as "Oslomarka", an area populated with moose, lynx, roe deer, and even the odd wolf, and legions of pine trees. A worthy tree is located by the head forester and space is cleared around it to allow light from all angles, and it is tended through the years to secure optimal growth.

Dec 17th – 23rd 1965

IN THE NEWS

Friday 17 — **"Maximum Security"** A machine gun has been fitted to Durham jail's roof, with a second variation issued to the soldiers guarding three of the great train robbers. The added precautions come following a report by the Ministry of Defence that the group who may try to free the criminals, have a force of over 100 men.

Saturday 18 — **"HMS Seraph"** A Secret Service Second World War submarine, HMS Seraph, made an adventurous final journey to a breakers' yard in Swansea. The submarine broke away while under tow in the English Channel, spending 24 hours drifting off Land's End.

Sunday 19 — **"Miserable Sinners"** The self-confessed 'miserable sinners' may have to change their 300-year-old practices following plans by the Archbishop of Canterbury to cut the General Confession from 133 words to 48.

Monday 20 — **"Stop and Test Measures"** The RAC have said that the random breathalyser checks are an '*unjustifiable interference*' with the rights of drivers who do not drink heavily.

Tuesday 21 — **"Keep Your Hat On"** Lady Burton of Coventry was present in the House of Lords wearing a high black 'Pilgrim Father's' hat to hear the House accept a recommendation from the Committee of Procedure, that peeresses who wish to wear a hat whilst speaking, should be allowed to do so.

Wednesday 22 — **"Moors Murders"** At the end of an 11-day moors murder case hearing, Ian Brady and Myra Hindley have been committed to trial by Cheshire Magistrates for the murders of three children.

Thursday 23 — **"Bollywood Cinema"** The 2,500 strong Indian Workers' Association are in negotiations to purchase the recently closed Dominion Cinema in Southall to screen '*Bollywood films*'.

HERE IN BRITAIN

"Hydrocar"

A British designed amphibious car, capable of 70mph on land and 30 knots on water is into its final stages of testing on the River Thames. The machine was invented by British designer, Charles Vinten, and is set to be displayed at this years' Boat Show.

It will go on sale in Britain for £3,500, though it is mainly intended for international export to areas where there are few bridges or frequent flooding. Currently powered by a 1500cc Porsche engine, Mr Vinten intends for the vehicle to eventually be an all-British product, including engine and assembly.

AROUND THE WORLD

"Rhodesia Embargo"

The Government has prohibited all British companies from supplying oil or oil products to Rhodesia. Supplying means a fine of £500 or six-months imprisonment.

The legislation, set to be supported by other European countries, is hoped to prevent the supply of oil to the port of Beira, and subsequently the use of the oil pipeline between Beira and Umtali, currently operated by a British subsidiary company. Separate provisions have been agreed to facilitate a continuous airlift of oil into Zambia by the Royal Air Force.

Keeping The Circus Alive

A sea lion balancing a large, striped ball on its nose is impressive, yes, entertaining, absolutely, but is it art? The 'art' of circus performance is to be put to the test by Bertram Mills Circus, who are considering applying to the Arts Council for a grant in the hope that it might save them from almost certain bankruptcy. All the acts of the travelling circus were sold at auction this summer, and the farewell performance this December is a combination of clowns, elephants and artistes from foreign acts. The suggestion has gained a lot of traction in recent weeks, and the Chairman of the Arts Council says he is still waiting on a proposition from the circus before a formal procedure can take place. The council already supports puppet shows in the Highlands, exhibitions of Anatolian antiquities, recitations of poetry in Penge, and other exotic and extravagant acts, so it is thought that the circus *'a tremendous vehicle for propaganda',* could easily fit alongside the already eccentric list.

The circus as we know it was born in 1768, when Newcastle-Under-Lyme born Philip Astley started showcasing events of horse trick riding in an open field just south of the River Thames. A skilled horse rider himself, by 1790, Astley began hiring acrobats, tightrope walkers, jugglers and a clown to fill the time between the equestrian demonstrations. The performance soon became known as a 'circus'.

Over the next fifty years, the style, format and settings of Astley's original performance developed. The ringmaster became a feature in the late 19th Century, as theatrical performances and choreographed musical acts became a staple of the performance. The original events were held in open aired structures with limited seating, it wasn't until the 1850s when the 'big-top tents', synonymous with the modern circus, were introduced.

Dec 24th – 31st 1965

IN THE NEWS

Friday 24 — **"Jets Prohibited from Refuelling"** All British Airways aircraft have been informed that no jet fuel will be available at Salisbury Airport, Rhodesia.

Saturday 25 — **"Christmas Broadcast"** The Queen delivered her annual Christmas broadcast from Buckingham Palace, embracing this years' theme of 'family'.

Sunday 26 — **"Boxing Day Hunts"** Several peaceful protests were staged by members of the League Against Animal Cruel Sports at Boxing Day hunts across the country, with as many as 80 people at each location

Monday 27 — **"Sea Gem Collapse"** British Petroleum's giant oil-rig *Sea-Gem* collapsed in the North Sea, killing at least four of the thirty-two men on board.

Tuesday 28 — **"BBC Cutbacks"** The BBC announced major cutbacks on building programmes in London, saving millions of pounds. The planned television centre at Whitehall will not be completed until more money is available.

Wednesday 29 — **"Floodlit Abbey"** Westminster Abbey will be floodlit for the first time from today to celebrate the start of the Abbey's 900th anniversary celebrations.

Thursday 30 — **"Circus Saved"** A London financier has come to the rescue of the Bertram Mills Circus Company, acquiring 69% for £145,000. It is hoped that this investment will help keep the circus performing for years to come.

Friday 31 — **"New Year's Eve"** This year amongst the revellers in Trafalgar Square, there was a clash between bathers and youths with beer tins and rolls of lavatory paper.

HERE IN BRITAIN

"Air-Rail Race"

Eight commuters raced from the Metropole Hotel in Brighton to the Jiffy Bar at Victoria Station. Half caught the 08:15am train to Victoria, while the others headed to Preston Park for a helicopter. Owing to bad weather, the helicopter was delayed, meaning that the train team entered the bar over an hour before the helicopter, but *both* claimed victory. The helicopter team's travel time was 14 minutes less, taking 1 hour 11 minutes; this was disregarded by the rail-goers, who argued that they arrived first. Eventually, both teams agreed on an honourable draw.

AROUND THE WORLD

"Life in Space"

The four American astronauts involved in the rendezvous of the *Gemini 6* and *Gemini 7* space capsules mid-orbit gave their personal accounts of life in space during a press conference at the Houston Space Centre. The *Gemini 6* capsule Captain, Walter Schirra, recalled how *'once we had got our confidence up'* they edged to within a foot of *Gemini 7*. The encounter was made whilst travelling at around 17,500mph, and came as a test for the Apollo moon landing expeditions scheduled for the end of the decade, when this kind of manoeuvre will be required.

He's Behind You!

The Christmas Pantomime

The Players' Theatre production of the famous pantomime 'Ali Baba', or '39 Thieves' opened with resounding success. One critic described the performance as a *'Sparkling success'*, with another commenting that it is *'not so much a revival, more a blood transfusion'*. Characterised by fantastic music, comedic brilliance and odes to the traditional performance, the 102-year-old story, is one of the best-known pantomime performances and this years' iteration is no disappointment.

The origins of pantomime date back to the 16th Century, where evidence of stock characters of a similar vein to modern day pantomimes could be found in Italian theatres. By the 18th Century, this had migrated to London's stages, where early pantomimes told classical stories using the original Italian stock characters. The Harlequin became the star of London pantomime, and the first Harlequin, John Rich, used his fortune to construct the Covent Garden Theatre, now a prominent feature of the London theatre scene. 'Harlequinades' - love stories full of slapstick humour and mimed to music, dominated the pantomime for over 100 years, until the Drury Lane Theatre implemented a speaking Harlequin and started writing pantomimes based on old English folk stories. Dick Whittington, Robin Hood and Babes in The Wood became household stories through theatre, and soon domestic culture and satire became a key theme of the pantomime, attracting enthusiastic audiences. The Victorian Pantomime, as this became known, changed the industry forever. Gone were mimes and classic stories, in favour of satire and slapstick, with the retention of a now stock character of a women authority figure played by a man.

1965 Calendar

January
S	M	T	W	T	F	S
					1	2
3	4	5	6	7	8	9
10	11	12	13	14	15	16
17	18	19	20	21	22	23
24	25	26	27	28	29	30
31						

February
S	M	T	W	T	F	S
	1	2	3	4	5	6
7	8	9	10	11	12	13
14	15	16	17	18	19	20
21	22	23	24	25	26	27
28						

March
S	M	T	W	T	F	S
	1	2	3	4	5	6
7	8	9	10	11	12	13
14	15	16	17	18	19	20
21	22	23	24	25	26	27
28	29	30	31			

April
S	M	T	W	T	F	S
				1	2	3
4	5	6	7	8	9	10
11	12	13	14	15	16	17
18	19	20	21	22	23	24
25	26	27	28	29	30	

May
S	M	T	W	T	F	S
						1
2	3	4	5	6	7	8
9	10	11	12	13	14	15
16	17	18	19	20	21	22
23	24	25	26	27	28	29
30	31					

June
S	M	T	W	T	F	S
		1	2	3	4	5
6	7	8	9	10	11	12
13	14	15	16	17	18	19
20	21	22	23	24	25	26
27	28	29	30			

July
S	M	T	W	T	F	S
				1	2	3
4	5	6	7	8	9	10
11	12	13	14	15	16	17
18	19	20	21	22	23	24
25	26	27	28	29	30	31

August
S	M	T	W	T	F	S
1	2	3	4	5	6	7
8	9	10	11	12	13	14
15	16	17	18	19	20	21
22	23	24	25	26	27	28
29	30	31				

September
S	M	T	W	T	F	S
			1	2	3	4
5	6	7	8	9	10	11
12	13	14	15	16	17	18
19	20	21	22	23	24	25
26	27	28	29	30		

October
S	M	T	W	T	F	S
					1	2
3	4	5	6	7	8	9
10	11	12	13	14	15	16
17	18	19	20	21	22	23
24	25	26	27	28	29	30
31						

November
S	M	T	W	T	F	S
	1	2	3	4	5	6
7	8	9	10	11	12	13
14	15	16	17	18	19	20
21	22	23	24	25	26	27
28	29	30				

December
S	M	T	W	T	F	S
			1	2	3	4
5	6	7	8	9	10	11
12	13	14	15	16	17	18
19	20	21	22	23	24	25
26	27	28	29	30	31	

IF YOU ENJOYED THIS BOOK PLEASE LEAVE A RATING OR REVIEW AT AMAZON

Printed in Great Britain
by Amazon

0d2128a3-203c-4591-a79c-5da5a77e1d44R01